PANIC CURE:

Poetry from Spain for the 21st Century

Panic Cure:

POETRY FROM SPAIN

for the

21ST CENTURY

Edited and translated by Forest Gander, and
with an Introduction by Daniel Aguirre-Oteiza

OTIS BOOKS | SEISMICITY EDITIONS

The Graduate Writing program
Otis College of Art and Design
LOS ANGELES ● 2014

Book design and typesetting: Rebecca Chamlee

ISBN-13: 978-0-9860173-4-6
ISBN: 0-9860173-4-5

OTIS BOOKS | SEISMICITY EDITIONS
The Graduate Writing program
Otis College of Art and Design
9045 Lincoln Boulevard
Los Angeles, CA 90045

www.otis.edu/graduate-writing/seismicity-editions
seismicity@otis.edu

For Aurelio Major & Juan Soros

Table of Contents

"No Remedy for My Ills":

SPANISH POETRY BEYOND GENERATIONAL BOUNDARIES

An Introduction

Panic Cure selects poems by "eleven innovative contemporary poets from Spain" writing in Spanish. It is not a comprehensive survey of national poetry, but rather a highly personal miscellany chosen by a non-Spanish poet, published outside of Spain, and created primarily for non-Spanish readers. The selection justifies itself by its peculiar foreignness: its guiding principle is Forrest Gander's understanding of innovation, as defined by his acute ear as an American translator who seeks out the restless, inquiring voices now proliferating that unbounded linguistic space many Mexican and US poets are creating as we speak. It is with this ear that Gander has chosen a small group of up-and-coming poets from Spain who unselfconsciously display a multiplicity of stylistic and procedural choices beyond constraints of national and generational identifications. Many of them are translators of unfixed abode. Yet they share with Antonio Gamoneda, Olvido García Valdés, and Miguel Casado–the three established voices that open the selection–a space of writing marked by non-linear, disjunctive, de-centered, multivocal, self-reflexive, linguistic acts. Truly individual poets and poems defamiliarize the reader's general sense of identity and affiliation in any history. A bilingual anthology only increases defamiliarization: as Miguel Casado argues, translation is "an experience of foreignness."

Foreign outlooks have generally been beneficial to criticism of recent Spanish poetry. In 1998, Andrew Debicki offered two reasons for this: the development of critical methods in the United States which were "hardly familiar to the Spanish literary establishment," and, secondly, the necessary distance from the

Spanish scene, which enabled the critic to "develop insights without getting trapped by personal considerations and by a mass of texts and writers." What Debicki saw as a "rich, varied, and turbulent poetic production" in late twentieth century Spain took place in a highly fraught cultural context which complicated the "simple analytic reading of texts and poets." A few words about the main characteristics of this national context may help clarify the relevance of a bilingual, "foreign" selection such as *Panic Cure*.

"With or without you, there is no remedy for my ills," says a popular song in Spanish. A new anthology of contemporary poets from Spain may strike readers interested in Spanish poetry as ill-fated. At least since 1932, when *Poesía española: Antología, 1915–1931* started the canonization process for the so-called *Generación del 27*–including poets as singular as Federico García Lorca and Luis Cernuda–, poetry anthologies have become a powerful tool for the consolidation of literary history in Spain. This history tends to tell a coherent national narrative following a continuous, chronological line marked by consecutive generational periods.[1] Whether in agreement or not with this conception of literary history, most anthologies of Spanish poetry published in the late twentieth century seemed to be entangled in a peculiar family romance. A family romance involves questions about one's identity and affiliation in a supposedly imposed, conflicting history. Even poetry collections not published in Spain–and therefore, in principle, less bound to stake out their position in the official family history–were sometimes unable to elude generational approaches. Since Spanish poets and critics appeared to be fatally "influenced by particular cultural traits," they "always embraced a spirit of belonging even if they saw themselves as unique individuals in conflict with the artistic 'generational manifesto' of their peers."[2] A generational approach has had ill effects on the study of poetry insofar as it has blurred the diversity of individual poets and poems in the interests of a particular linguistic, national,

---

1 See Epps and Fernández Cifuentes.

2 Ramos-García.

and historical identity. This ill afflicts all readers interested in innovative poets and poems. One possible remedy for it may lie beyond the margins of national poetry collections by Spanish readers–including introductions such as this one.

Literary history was further consolidated in Spain by the highly institutionalized scene of late twentieth century Spanish poetry. A long-standing controversy about the conditions of possibility of poetic tradition and canon-formation complicated the dissemination of individual poetic voices. Anthologies proliferated in the midst of controversy, and, whether included or not in them, new poems and poets seemed subordinated to the embattled development of monumental literary history. Even Spanish critics who conceived of poems as a multiplicity of heterogeneous and even conflicting, "untimely" linguistic acts, sounded at times a justificatory note in the face of a polarized poetry scene: "This is an anthology of diversity. I never wanted to make an anthology against or in favor of anything, except for the works of the poets themselves."[3] These notes appeared as symptoms of a sort of anxiety of anthological confluence, as if proclamations of difference or disaffiliation could fatally confirm and reinforce the continuity of the single linear tradition established by literary history.[4]

Since its inception in 1980, the massive, canon-oriented, and now indispensable work of scholarly reference *Historia y crítica de la literatura española* has generally classified poets according

---

3 Méndez.

4 The foreword to Las ínsulas extrañas (2002), an important controversial collection published in Spain covering poets the whole Spanish-speaking world, sounds this justificatory note, albeit in a more aggressive fashion, against the allegedly "pseudo-realist dogma" prevalent in late 20th century Spanish poetry. Poetas en blanco y negro (2004), another important collection covering poets from the whole Spanish-speaking world, is advertised in negative terms: "This is not an anthology, but just an invitation to poetry. It is not a book aiming at influencing the 'poetry world.' Its ambition is not to mark a canon, it does not defend a particular school, it does not want to make the picture of a generation, it does not keep 'enough perspective', it does not aspire to systematize anything."

to national generations, schools, trends, etc.[5] In 2000, the editor of the supplement to the ninth volume described his project as "maybe excessively traditional." Far from addressing revolts, breaks, or inflections admittedly happening in contemporary Spanish literature–not to mention related cultural practices in other Spanish languages and Spanish-speaking countries–, the supplement, significantly titled *Los nuevos nombres: 1975–2000*, aimed at tracing "a basic continuity between story-tellers and poets who started developing a new moral, literary, aesthetic, and political coherence in Spain between the fifties and today." Furthermore, although some critics insisted on the need to read poets and poems individually–"Spanish poetry as a group does not exist.... A true poet can never *represent* the poetry of others"–, the critical framework outlined in the supplement sweepingly assimilated proposals for different critical methods as mere signs of the vitality of the contemporary Spanish poetry scene.[6]

Today most Spanish criticism of poetry is still denounced for a normative method that emphasizes commonalities and conventions over singularities and innovations for the sake of classification and coherence.[7] As Julián Jiménez Heffernan contends, there are two "histories" of poetry in Spanish. "External history" is the consistent chronology established by philology and literary history. By contrast, "internal history" is anachronistic–it is, in fact, a non-history: a conflicting depository of poetic lines surviving in poets' and readers' memories in a sort of persistent non-contemporaneity beyond national and generational boundaries. The "internal history" of poems diverges from conventional literary history in manifold ways. Non-teleological, it is not "a continuous and progressive incorporation of the past,"

<hr>

5 This critical practice has important, "historical" precedents: Juan Luis Alborg's *Historia de la literatura española* (1975) and Felipe B. Pedraza's and Milagros Rodríguez's *Manual de literatura española* (1980).

6 See Pedro Provencio and Miguel Casado in "La pregunta or la poesía: Apuntes para trazar un marco," included in Casado's *Los artículos de la polémica*.

7 Casado, "Sobre historia, crítica y poética en la poesía española contemporánea."

but as "errant movement whose present is troubled by a retrace that it never articulates once and for all."[8] In this sense, a poem is experienced as an ever-new linguistic act in conflict with the current common use of language. It is a multi-vocal self-reflexive discourse where identity is perceived as precarious. In Olvido García Valdés' words: "It cuts off and expands and a moment / blooms before the wounding. Rhythms / of respiration and the sky, one / place among others, a volume / that anyone who breathes-in gives back." Beyond this binary, a third history would problematize external and internal histories in an attempt to pose a critique of social languages whereby literary history becomes a tool for perceiving ways of socio-historical translformation.

Innovation is the generic term that defines this anthology. For the reader of poetry in English, this term will harken back to Ezra Pound's modernist slogan, "make it new." To the reader of poetry in Spanish, it may bring to mind Octavio Paz's take on a larger, transnational family romance: the fraught relation between Latin American and Spanish poetry. According to the Mexican poet, Ezra Pound's dictum defines modern poetry as both a rejection and an extension of the tradition inaugurated by Romanticism – a self-critical tradition that "seeks continuity through rejection." In the late '60s and early '70s, this synoptic view of modernity as a "tradition against itself" was Paz's way of mapping modern poetry in Spanish. *Modernismo* and the avant-garde were imported to Spain by Nicaraguan Rubén Darío and Chilean Vicente Huidobro, respectively, whereas early twentieth century Spanish poets such as Unamuno, Antonio Machado, Juan Ramón Jiménez, and García Lorca tended to bathe both aesthetic revolutions in tradition. While a sense of uprootedness and orphanhood in Latin America encouraged an impulse toward cultural cosmopolitanism and linguistic adventurousness, a strong sense of a national past prevented most Spanish poets from incorporating the radical cultural and linguistic challenges defining the poetics of modernity. In *Latin American* modernity, the will to change helped

8   See Cox.

sustain a multicultural condition in constant transition. In *Spanish* modernity, the will to change generally implied revisiting and reinforcing a well-established national tradition.

Although Paz may have seemed overly prone to setting up binary discriminations when he explored identity issues characteristic of family romances, his complex and dynamic view of literary history also acknowledged Latin American problematic aesthetic nationalism and parochialism, as well as the exceptional searching modernity of Juan Ramón Jiménez's prose poem *Espacio*. More importantly, his insistent self-interrogations provided the reader of poetry with much-needed insights into how and why the heterogeneous, discontinuous, and self-critical elements of modernity were largely resisted by critics in Spain. [9] Paz denounced the Spanish academic critic who routinely "seeks in modern writers an extension of those traits that seem to him characteristic of the tradition of *his literature*." The idea of a Spanish national tradition defined by a set of constant features such as "realism" or "mysticism" can only distort the reception of innovative poetry. But, as Paz warned, there is nothing more absurd than trying to domesticate the work of a poet as intellectually and geographically restless as Luis Cernuda into the general category of "Spanish" poetry.

The conservatism of this critical attitude can still be traced in recent Spanish scholarship on Spanish poetry. Significantly, in the twenty-first century, Cernuda's poetry and criticism still constitute one of the most contested legacies among contemporary Spanish writers. For critics who believe that high-sounding rhetoric is another constant (negative) feature of Spanish poetry, Cernuda became an example of the way in which late twentieth century Spanish poets could renovate tradition. His late poetry

---

9 This robust critical binarism can still be detected nowadays. An idiosyncratic critical attempt at dismantling traditionalism in Spanish poetry was Agustín Fernández Mallo's long essay *Postpoesía* (2009). The Mexican cultural magazine *Letras Libres* benevolently dismissed it as a regional querelle "between ancients and moderns (or postmoderns and late-postmoderns or whatever) within a national literature." For a reader of recent Latin American poetry such as Alejandro Zambra, this essay about the "stagnation" of Spanish poetry sounded "very old."

and criticism showed how certain poetic conventions helped develop the language of the social contract into a "natural," "normal," broadly accessible poem–as opposed to the allegedly self-marginalizing linguistic disjointedness of new avant-garde poetic projects of the seventies. For other critics, however, Cernuda's late works are examples of high-sounding rhetoric precisely because they illustrate a self-legitimizing attempt to inscribe his poetry in conventional literary historiography.[10]

Traits of this conservatism may be easily recognized by the American reader. In 1991, Marjorie Perloff decried a New Formalism in American poetry that, against the supposedly exhausted innovations of mid-century poetics, promoted a narrative poem with identifiable locales and consistent characters, singing "in a natural, not puffed up, way so that one can reach an audience." Refusing to make apocalyptic generalizations about the "end of art," Perloff challenged claims that avant-garde experiments were a thing of the past, and proposed a redefinition of critical parameters that may explore, in Charles Bernstein's words, "a fragmentation that reflects a conception of meaning as prevented by conventional narration and so uses disjunction as a method of tapping into other possibilities available within language." In 1983, Bernstein had polemically defined the "officially sanctioned verse" of our time as characterized by "a restricted vocabulary, neutral and univocal tone in the guise of voice or persona, grammar-book syntax, received conceits, static and unitary form." Very broadly speaking, this *retour à l'ordre* can be traced to W. H. Auden's anti-avant-garde legacy in late twentieth century American and Spanish poetry. In Spain, the conservative bent of this legacy lay in "its subordination of both aesthetic and political concerns to the norm of social decorum."[11] Worryingly, linguistic disjointedness was taken as a symbol of a failed social contract, and modernist art summarily equated to dictatorial politics. Despite its claims to inclusiveness, the new poetics was exclusionary or reductive

---

10 See Jiménez Heffernan.

11 Mayhew, "The Avant-Garde and Its Discontents."

inasmuch as it sweepingly situated all avant-gardist breaks with the past within a "homogenizing and negative political movement," while identifying itself with the "normalized" poetry industry of the new democratic Spain. [12]

This broad critical framework, triangulating between Latin American, Spanish, and US poets, may help explain why it is pertinent that Antonio Gamoneda should open *Panic Cure*. Gamoneda's poetry shares some key elements with Bernstein's description of innovative poetics. Bernstein contends that "normalcy is the enemy of poetry," while Gamoneda champions an "abnormal language ... in which what is said is unsayable in 'everyday' language." Instead of conveying emotions or ideas, poetry lets "language find ways of meaning" through the poet, and "the music of poetry is the sound of sense coming to be in the world," says Bernstein. In a similar vein, Gamoneda believes that "the activity of memory and of thought is subsequent to a musical impulse," and only the "radical reality" created by writing makes thought "sensitive/intelligible" to the poet. The poet only knows what he is saying when it has already been said.

In 1999, Gamoneda identified two main trends among Spanish poets under fifty years of age: "mini-realism" and "radical realism." Allowing for wide-ranging differences within each field, Gamoneda schematically differentiated between an institutional, conventional, communicative, "informative" poetics, and a self-critical, exploratory, language-oriented poetics. "Mini-realist" poets propounded the articulation of "data" extracted from daily life by means of a colloquial, "normalized" language. They showed a fondness for ornamental diction couched in "legitimate" metrical, rhyming, and stanzaic patterns; an aversion to avant-garde or transgressive poetics projects both in Spain and in Latin America (such as those of Huidobro, Larrea, Lorca, Neruda, and Vallejo, from which they tended to carefully incorporate only "usable" elements); and scant interest in contemporary poetry in other languages. Gamoneda was at his most combative – and perhaps also at his most reductive – when

---

12 García Montero.

drawing political analogies: he suggested that "mini-realism" was to neo-capitalism as Socialist-realism was to institutional Communism–both were sterile, academic poetic modes. Furthermore, "mini-realism" was consistent with the post-Francoist political establishment–regardless of the poets' ideological sympathies–, and, specifically, with key elements in the current poetry industry: text-books published with public money, awards judged by individuals working in major trade publishers and universities, presses connected with corporations, government departments, mainstream critics, etc. As Jonathan Mayhew has argued, "political, educational, and literary institutions converge[d] in order to overdetermine the premature canonization" of poetic schools in Spain.

The entrenched debate about the relation between late twentieth century "official" verse and innovative poetics broadly described by Gamoneda and Bernstein may seem dated today. Gamoneda is now probably as much a respected and controversial figure as the central spokesmen of "mini-realism" whom he chastises. A similar claim could be made about Bernstein. More importantly, "official" poetry industries may be losing sway in the rapidly-changing cultural field of current Spanish poetry: new anthologies and technologies are mapping a more open, flexible, and unselfconscious scene where multiple individual voices are being disseminated beyond the homogenizing constraints set by academic categories such as school, generation and nation, or more generally, by a cultural field that tends to promote self-protective, self-isolating strategies for institutionalization.[13]

All-inclusive anthologies are in themselves an oxymoron. As a response to exclusionary selections, they tend to follow a compensatory principle conditioned by the disjunctive, either/or logic dominating entrenched poetry scenes. This bilingual selection entails at least two specific linguistic interventions–it introduces a limited group of little-known contemporary Spanish poets to American readers interested in innovative writing beyond debates about official and non-official verse cultures.

13 See, for instance, Moga's Poesía Pasión. Also, http://www.7de7.net/home.php and http://criticadepoesia.blogspot.com. For strategies, see Labrador.

Furthermore, it is an invitation to leave the comfort zone of literary histories; it affords an alternative view of domestic poetic discourses of any persuasion. Beyond personal preferences, the discursive displacement specific to translation alters the all-too-familiar either/or debates dominating national poetry scenes. In this light, *Panic Cure* may contribute to opening up the largely inbred industry of modern Spanish poetry, if only because its readers will be hard put to consider it yet another attempt at settling family quarrels. Gander's anthology is not circumscribed by national debates about aesthetic normativity and normalization. Significantly, his previous editorial work includes the publication of bilingual writer Mónica de la Torre's magisterial translation of the poems of Gerardo Deniz, Mexico's *novateur extraordinaire*, who still awaits proper recognition in his native country, Spain. Significantly enough, the title of Gerardo Deniz's complete poetry, *Erdera*, is Basque for "foreign language."

Beyond domestic recognition in Spain, perhaps the poems selected by Forrest Gander needed to be literally foreignized (both from "home" and from their linguistic "body") in order to be recognized as what they are—voices speaking uncannily "abnormal" languages. *Panic Cure* displaces—yet again—Olvido García Valdés' disturbing voice: "Another country, another landscape, / another city. / An unknown place / and an unknown body, / your own body, strange / road leading / straight into dread." This "dread" points to the ambivalent title: *Panic Cure* can be a cure for panic and a cure by panic. In this sense, it is not a remedy, but it may bring relief to poets trying to open unpredictable poetic itineraries within a "tradition against itself," beyond debates about the linear traditions established by literary history.

— *Daniel Aguirre-Oteiza, Harvard University, 2012*

Bernstein, Charles. *My Way: Speeches and Poems.* Chicago: University of Chicago Press, 1999.

Content's Dream: Essays 1975–1984. Los Angeles, Calif.: Sun & Moon Press, 1986.

Casado, Miguel. *Los artículos de la polémica y otros textos sobre poesía.* Madrid: Biblioteca Nueva, c2005.

La experiencia de lo extranjero: ensayos sobre poesía. Barcelona: Galaxia Gutenberg: Círculo de Lectores, 2009.

"Sobre historia, crítica y poética en la poesía española contemporánea." *Veinte poetas españoles del siglo xx.* Ed. Marta López-Luaces. Caracas: Fundación Editorial el perro y la rana. 2008.

Cox, Christoph. "The (End of the) End of History." *The Ends of Theory.* Ed. Jerry Herron. Detroit: Wayne State University Press, 1996.

Debicki, Andrew. "Criticism and Poetic Creation." *Revista de Estudios Hispánicos.* Vol. 32, No. 3, 1998.

Deniz, Gerardo. *Poemas = Poems.* Ed. and trans., Mónica de la Torre. México, D.F. : Ditoria/Lost Roads Publishers, 2000.

Diego, Gerardo, ed. *Poesía española: Antología, 1915–1931.* Madrid, Editorial Signo, 1932.

Epps, Brad, and Luis Fernández Cifuentes, eds. *Spain Beyond Spain: Modernity, Literary History, and National Identity.* Lewisburg: Bucknell University Press, 2005.

Gamoneda, Antonio. *El cuerpo de los símbolos.* Madrid: Huerga & Fierro Editores, 1997.

"¿Poesía en los años 2000?". *La alegría de los naufragios,* No. 1 and 2. Madrid: Huerga & Fierro Editores, 1999.

García Montero, Luis. *Confesiones poéticas.* Granada: Excma. Diputación Provincial de Granada, 1993.

Gracia, Jordi, ed. *Historia y crítica de la literatura española. Primer suplemento: Los nuevos nombres: 1975–2000.* Madrid: Crítica, 2000.

Iglesias, Amalia. *Poetas en blanco y negro.* Madrid: Abada, 2006.

Jiménez Heffernan, Julián, *Los papeles rotos: ensayos de poesía española contemporánea.* Madrid: Abada, 2004.

Mayhew, Jonathan. "The Avant-Garde and Its Discontents: Aesthetic Conservatism in Recent Spanish Poetry." *Hispanic Review*, Vol. 67, No. 3, 1999.

"Poetry, politics, and power" *Journal of Spanish Cultural Studies*, Vol. 3, No. 2, 2002.

Méndez, José, ""'La prueba del nueve' recopila la diversidad de la poesía española actual." *El País*. 4 February 1995. Web. 15 December 2010.

Milán, Eduardo [et al.], ed. *Las ínsulas extrañas: antología de poesía en lengua española (1950–2000)*. Barcelona : Galaxia Gutenberg: Círculo de Lectores, 2002.

Labrador, Germán. "Sin novedad en el parnaso. Teoría y práctica del discurso poético en el campo literario actual." *Hesperia: Anuario de Filología Hispánica*. No. 9, 2006.

Moga, Eduardo, ed. *Poesía pasión*. Zaragoza : Libros del Innombrable, 2004.

Paz, Octavio. *Obras completas I: La casa de la presencia (poesía e historia). (Dominio hispánico)*. Barcelona : Galaxia Gutenberg: Círculo de Lectores, 1999.

Obras Completas II: Excursiones / Incursiones (dominio extranjero). Fundación y disidencia. Barcelona : Galaxia Gutenberg: Círculo de Lectores, 1999.

Perloff, Marjorie. *Radical artifice: Writing Poetry in the Age of Media*. Chicago: University of Chicago Press, 1991.

Ramos-García, Luis A., ed. *A Bilingual Anthology of Spanish Poetry: The Generation of 1970*. Trans. Dave Oliphant. Introd. Miguel Casado. Lewiston, N.Y.: Edwin Mellen Press, 1997.

Zambra, Alejandro, "Post-poesía: hacia un nuevo paradigma, de Agustín Fernández-Mallo." *Letras Libres*. August 2009. Web. 15 December 2010.

A poet, I've been turned on to poetry in Spain by other poets, by reading books and literary journals, and by going to readings and bookstores in Barcelona, Madrid, Sevilla, Bilbao, and Valencia over the last two decades. This anthology charts some of my own enthusiasms; it isn't a comprehensive list. It seems more significant to represent eleven substantial writers with a generous selection of poems than thirty or forty writers with one or two poems apiece. The eleven poets collected here represent one of many possible configurations of an exploratory surge that signals a moment of change in Spain's literature. Another anthology I might have put together would include work by Oscar Curieses, Jordi Doci, Marta Lopez-Luaces, Elena Medel, Antonio Masoliver, Carlos Pardo, and Eduardo Moga. Other poets in Spain, writing in Spanish, Galician, Catalan, Asturian, and Basque might have been included. *Feroces*, a Spanish anthology of "radical, marginal, and heterodoxical" recent poetries bears mention, although no writers included in that anthology are included in this one. *New Poetry from Spain*, edited by Marta López-Luaces, Johnny Lorenz, and Edwin M. Lamboy is another worth discovering. After stepping clear of a long dictatorship, after elections and new freedoms in Spain, every person and certainly every artist faces the question of what comes next. There is the panic of the blank page, the 21st century, a transformed and transforming world. And there is the cure, the curandero-poet, the vivifying impulse.

Panic Cure

Antonio Gamoneda

Antonio Gamoneda was born in Oviedo in 1931. His father was a modernist poet whose career was cut short by his early death. The young Antonio reputedly learned to read, during the Spanish Civil War when schools were closed, by immersing himself in his father's poems. His own first book, *Sublevación inmóvil*, published in 1960, was a runner-up for the Adonais Prize. Working with progressive cultural organizations, Gamoneda didn't publish another book of poems until after the fall of Franco. Then, in 1977, he published the impressive long poem *Descripción de la mentira* (León 1977). After that followed *Lápidas* (Madrid, 1987) and *Edad*, which won the National Prize for Literature in Spain. In 1992, *Libro del frío* was published. An expanded and revised version included *Frío de límites*, a collaboration with the artist Antoni Tàpies. *Arden las pérdidas* was published in 2003 and *La luz*, a new collected poetry (1947–2004) was published in 2004. In 2006, Gamoneda was awarded the Reina Sofia Award and the Cervantes Prize, the highest honors in Spanish literature.

de *Arden las perdidas*

Ira

DE LAS violentas humedades, de
los lugares donde se entrecruzan
residuos de tormentas y sollozos,
viene
esta pena arterial, esta memoria
despedazada.
              Aún enloquecen
aquellas madres en mis venas.

*

HASTA los signos vienen
las sombras torturadas.
Pienso en el día en que los caballos aprendieron a llorar.

Rage

FROM the violent drizzle, from
places where residues
of torments and sobs mesh,
comes
this arterial grief, this shredded
memory.
            They drive insane
even those mothers who course through in my veins.

*

THE TORTURED shadows
approach the signs.
I think about the day when horses learned to weep.

¿QUIÉN viene
dando gritos, anuncia
aquel verano, enciende
lámparas negras, silba
en la pureza azul de los cuchillos?

*

VIENEN con lámparas, conducen

serpientes ciegas a

las arenas albarizas.

Hay un incendio de campanas. Se

oye gemir el acero

en la ciudad rodeada de llanto.

WHO shows up
shouting, announcing
a summer like this, lighting
black lamps, hissing
into the pure blue of knives?

*

THEY COME with lanterns, lugging

blind snakes to

the albescent sand.

There's a blaze of bells. Steel

can be heard groaning

in the city walled by wailing.

GRITAN ante los muros calcinados.

Ven el perfil de los cuchillos, ven
el círculo del sol, la cirugía
del animal lleno de sombra.

                    Silban

en las fístulas blancas.

*

HUBO extracción de hombres. Vi

la raíz morada del augurio.

Vi a los insectos libando el llanto, vi

sangre en las iglesias amarillas

THEY SCREAM before calcined walls.

They note the silhouette of knives, see
the sun's circle, the surgery
of the animal stuffed with shadow.

They hiss

into white fistulas.

*

THERE WAS an extraction of men. I saw

the root living on the omen.

I saw insects sucking up tears, saw

blood splashed on the yellow churches.

HABÍA flores abrasadas, dril
sobre la máquina que llora.
Aceite y llanto en el acero y
hélices y números sangrientos
en la pureza de la ira.

*

CONOCÍ los sudarios habitados
y las bujías del dolor. Hervían
las oraciones en los labios
de las mujeres frías.

THERE were scorched flowers and denim

draped over a weeping machine.

Oil and wailing in the steel and

propellers and bloody numbers

in the purity of my rage.

*

I RECOGNIZED the tenanted shrouds

and the spark plugs of pain. Orations

boiled up between the lips

of shivering women.

FUE
la música mortal, el alarido
de los caballos incesantes, fue
una pavana fúnebre a la hora
del algodón ensangrentado.

Fue la declinación de mil cabezas,
la gárgola que aúlla maternal, los círculos
de la gallina atormentada.

Es aún, otra vez, la cal, el hueso
frío en nuestras manos, la
médula negra de la policía.

*

VI
cuerpos al borde de
las acequias frías.

Amortajados
en la luz.

IT WAS
mortal music, the shriek
of incessant horses, it was
a funeral pavane at the hour
of the bloodied cotton ball.

It was the drooping of thousands of heads,
the gargoyle, its maternal howl, the circles
of the tormented hen.

It's even, once again, the whitewash, the bone
cold in our hands, the
policeman's black marrow.

*

I SAW
bodies along the edge of
the cold acequias.

Shrouded
in light.

vi los alambres y las cuerdas, vi

la semilla del metal y el soto

blanco de espinos y de luz. Con púrpura

se alimentaban los insectos.

*

HALLÉ mercurio en las pupilas, lágrimas

en las maderas, luz

en la pared de los agonizantes.

I SAW the ropes and cords, saw

the metallic seed and the briars

white with spines and light. Enpurpled,

they were gobbling up the insects.

*

I FOUND mercury in my pupils, tears

in the lumber, light

at the wall of the dying.

BAJO la actividad de las hormigas

había párpados y había

agua mortal en las cunetas.

Aún en mi corazón

hay hormigas.

*

VA a amanecer sobre las cárceles y las tumbas.

Me mira la cabeza torturada: su

marfil arde como un relámpago cautivo.

BENEATH the busyness of ants

there were eyelids and there was

toxic water in the gutters.

Even in my heart

there are ants.

*

IT's going to dawn over the prisons and tombs.

The tortured head eyes me: its

ivory blazes like caught lightning.

Pavana Impura

1

Tu cabello en sus manos; arde en las manos del vigilante de la
   nieve.
Son las cebadas, la siesta de las serpientes y tu cabello en el
   pasado.
Abre tus ojos para que yo vea las cebadas blancas: tu cabeza en
   las manos del vigilante de la nieve.

2

Todos los árboles se han puesto a gemir dentro de mi espíritu al
   recordar tus bragas en la oscuridad, la luz debajo de tu piel,
   tus pétalos vivientes.
Atravesando los aniversarios, a veces viajan las palomas ebrias.
Venga desnuda tu misericordia, ah paloma mortal, hija del
   campo.

3

El mirlo en la incandescencia de tus labios se extingue.
Yo siento en ti grandes heridas y te desnudas en mis fuentes.
Se extingue el mirlo en las alcobas blancas donde soy ciego,
   donde, algunas veces, suenan en ti grandes campanas.

4

Busco tu piel inconfesable, tu piel ungida por la tristeza de las
   serpientes; distingo tus asuntos invisibles, el rastro frío del
   corazón.
Hubiera visto tu cinta ensangrentada, tu llanto entre cristales
y no tu llaga amarilla,

pero mi sueño vive debajo de tus párpados.

Impure Pavane

1

Your hair in his hands; burning in the vigilante's hands of snow.
It's barley grain, the nap of snakes and your hair in the past.
Open your eyes that I might see the white barley: your head in
    the vigilante's hands of snow.

2

The trees have all been moaning in my mind in remembrance
    of your panties in the darkness, the light under your skin,
    your living petals.
Crossing anniversaries, now and again, intoxicated pigeons fly
    past.
Come bare your mercy, ah mortal dove, daughter of the field.

3

The blackbird in the glow of your lips has blown out.
I can sense in you your impressive wounds, you bare yourself in
    my fountains.
The blackbird blows out in white bedrooms where I go blind,
    where, now and again, extravagant bells ring.

4

Feeling for your unconfessable skin, your skin anointed with
    the sadness of snakes; I can make out your invisible worries,
    your heart's cold trail.
I would have noticed your bloody sash, your weeping between
    window panes, and not the yellow of your wound,

but my dream lives under your eyelids.

5

La inexistencia es hueca como las máscaras y su visión es lívida,
    pero tú oyes el grito de las madres del agua y acaricias los
    ojos que vieron la inexistencia.

6

Nuestros cuerpos se comprenden cada vez más tristemente,
    pero yo amo esta púrpura desolada.
Ah la flor negra de los dormitorios, ah las pastillas del amanecer.

7

Entra otra vez en las alcobas blancas.
Grandes son las jarras de la tristeza en las manos mortales.
Entra otra vez en las alcobas blancas.

8

Amor que duras en mis labios:

Hay una miel sin esperanza bajo las hélices y las sombras de
    las grandes mujeres y en la agonía del verano baja como
    mercurio hasta la llaga azul del corazón.

Amor que duras: llora entre mis piernas,

come la miel sin esperanza.

5

Though oblivion is hollow as a mask, a livid apparition, you
hear the wailing of mothers from the water and you pet those
eyes that glimpsed oblivion.

6

Our bodies comprehend themselves with more and more
sadness, but I love this desolate purple.
Ah the black flower of bedrooms, ah the pills of dawn.

7

Enter the white bedroom once more.
Impressive, the jars of sadness in mortal hands.
Enter the white bedroom once more.

8

Love, that you last on my lips:

There's a forlorn honey in the helixes and shadows of impres-
sive women and in summer's agony it sinks like mercury
into the heart's blue gash.

Love, that you might last: cry between my thighs,

eat the forlorn honey.

9

Ha venido tu lengua; está en mi boca
como una fruta en la melancolía.
Ten piedad en mi boca: liba, lame,
amor mío, la sombra.

10

Llegan los animales del silencio, pero debajo de tu piel arde la
    amapola amarilla, la flor del mar ante los muros calcinados
    por el viento y el llanto.
Es la impureza y la piedad, el alimento de los cuerpos abando-
    nados por la esperanza.

11

He envejecido dentro de tus ojos; eras la dulzura y el exterminio
    y yo amé tu cuerpo en sus frutos nocturnos.
Tu inocencia es como un cuchillo delante de mi rostro,
pero tú pesas en mi corazón y, como una miel oscura, yo te
    siento en mis labios al ir hacia la muerte.

12

Eres como la flor de los agonizantes
que es invisible mas su aroma entra
en la sombra nasal y es la delicia,
todo en la vida, durante algún tiempo.

9

It's come, your tongue; in my mouth,
like fruit in gloom.
Have mercy on my mouth: suck, lick,
my love, at the shadow.

10

Animals materialize from silence, but under your skin a yellow
    poppy burns, the flower of the sea against walls calcined by
    tears and wind.
Impurity and piety, provisions for corpses hope has abandoned.

11

I've grown old in your eyes; you were the sweetness and the
    extermination and I loved your body, its nocturnal fruits.
Your innocence, like a knife at my face,
but you weigh down my heart and I feel you on my lips, like
    dark honey, as I go at my death.

12

You're like the flower of the dying,
invisible though your aroma lifts
into my nasal shadows as pure delight,
the whole of a life, in its time.

13
En la humedad me amas
y eres azul en tus pezones. hablas
suavemente en mis labios y regresas
a tu prisión en la melancolía.

14
Tu cabello encanece entre mis manos y, como aguas silen-
    ciosas, nos abandonan los recuerdos. siento la frialdad de la
    existencia pero tu olor se extiende en las habitaciones y tu
    lascivia vive en mi corazón y entra mi pensamiento en tus
    heridas.

15
Existe el mar en las ciudades blancas,
coágulos en el aire dulcemente sangriento,
sábanas en la serenidad.
Existen los perfumes inguinales, lenguas en las heridas
    femeninas
y el corazón está cansado.
Entra con tus campanas en mi casa, pastora ciega, sin embargo,
como si no tuviera la dulzura su fin aún en las ciudades blancas.

13

In the dampness you love me
and go blue in your nipples. Speaking
softly against my lips, then turning back
to your sullen prison.

14

Your hair greys in my hands and, quiet waters, our memories
give up on us. I feel the coldness of life but your scent seeps
through the rooms and your lust thrives in my heart and
dives into my thoughts through your wounds.

15

There's a sea in white cities,
clots in the sweet bloody air,
sheets in serenity.
There are inguinal perfumes, tongues in feminine wounds
and my heart tires out.
Bring your bells into my house, blind shepherdess, anyway,
as though sweetness might never cease in these white cities.

Diván en Nueva York

Tú en la tristeza de los urinarios, ante las cánulas de bronce
(amor, amor en las iglesias húmedas);
ah, sollozabas en las barberías (en los espejos, los agonizantes
estaban dentro de tus ojos):
así es el llanto.
Y aquellas madres amarillas en el hedor de la misericordia:
así es el llanto.
Ah de la obscenidad, ah del acero.

Vi las aguas coléricas, y sábanas, y, en los museos, junto a la
dulzura, vi los imanes de la muerte.
Te desnudaron en marfil (ancianas, en los prostíbulos
profundos) y te midieron en dolor, oscuro:
así es el llanto, así es el llanto.
Ten piedad de tus labios y de mi espíritu en los almacenes;
ten piedad del alcohol en los dormitorios iluminados.
Veo las delaciones, veo indicios: llagas azules en tu lengua,
números negros en tu corazón:

ah de los besos, ah de las penínsulas.

Así es el llanto;
así es el llanto y las serpientes están llorando en Nueva York.

Así es el llanto.

New York Divan

You in the sadness of the urinals, before brass cannulas
(love, love in damp churches);
ah, sobbing in barbershops (in mirrors, the dying
were there in your eyes):
so the crying.
And those sallow mothers caught up in mercy's stench:
so the crying.
Ah of the obscenity, ah of steel.

I saw choleric waters, and sheets, and, in museums, along with
the sweetness, I saw death's magnets.
They undressed you on ivory (old women, far back in the
brothels) and they measured you out in pain, in darkness:
so the crying, so the crying.
Have mercy on your lips and on my soul in the grocery stores;
have mercy on alcohol in the lit-up dormitories.
I see denunciations, I see signs: blue sores on your tongue,
black numbers in your heart:

ah of kisses, ah of peninsulas.

So the crying;
so the crying and the snakes are crying in New York.

So the crying.

Estar en ti

Yo no entro en ti para que tú te pierdas
bajo la fuerza de mi amor;
yo no entro en ti para perderme
en tu existencia ni en la mía;
yo te amo y actúo en tu corazón
para vivir con tu naturaleza,
para que tú te extiendas en mi vida.
Ni tú ni yo. Ni tú ni yo.
Ni tus cabellos esparcidos aunque los amo tanto.
Sólo esta oscura compañía. Ahora
siento la libertad. Esparce
tus cabellos. Esparce tus cabellos.

Being in You

I don't enter you so you lose yourself
under the force of my love;
I don't enter you to lose myself
in your life or mine;
I love you and I act in your heart
to live with you as you are,
that you might protract yourself in my life.
Not you not me. Not you not me.
Nor your hair spread out although I love it.
Only this unlit companionship. Now
I'm clear. Spread
your hair. Spread your hair.

[En la ebriedad le rodeaban mujeres...]

En la ebriedad le rodeaban mujeres, sombra, policía, viento.

Ponía venas en las urces cárdenas, vértigo en la pureza; la flor
furiosa de la escarcha era azul en su oído.

Rosas, serpientes y cucharas eran bellas mientras permanecían
en sus manos.

[Inebriated, he was surrounded by women...]

Inebriated, he was surrounded by women, shadow, police, wind.

He strung veins across the heather row, put the vertigo in virtue, frost's furious flower blossomed blue in his ear.

Roses, snakes and spoons were beautiful so long as he held them in his hands.

[Vigilaba la serenidad adherida a las sombras...]

Vigilaba la serenidad adherida a las sombras, los círculos donde se depositan flores abrasadas, la inclinación de los sarmientos.

Algunas tardes, su mano incomprensible nos conducía al lugar sin nombre, a la melancolía de las herramientas abandonadas.

[He noticed the calm clinging to shadows...]

He noticed the calm clinging to shadows, the circles where burnt flowers fell, the inclination of vines.

Some evenings, his incomprehensible hand pointed us to a nameless place, to the melancholy of abandoned tools.

[Un animal oculto...]

Un animal oculto en el crepúsculo me vigila y se apiada demí.
Pesan las frutas corrompidas, hierven las cámaras corporales.
Cansa atravesar esta enfermedad llena de espejos. Alguien
silba en mi corazón. No sé quién es pero entiendo su sílaba
interminable.

Hay sangre en mi pensamiento, escribo sobre lápidas negras.
Yo mismo soy el animal extraño. Me reconozco: lame los
párpados que ama, lleva en su lengua las sustancias paternales.
Soy yo, no hay duda: canta sin voz y se ha sentado a contemplar
la muerte, pero no ve más que lámparas y moscas y las leyendas
de las cintas fúnebres. A veces, grita en tardes inmóviles.

Lo invisible está dentro de la luz, pero, ¿arde algo dentro de lo
invisible? La imposibilidad es nuestra iglesia. En todo caso, el
animal se niega a fatigarse en la agonía.

Es el que está despierto en mí cuando yo duermo. No ha nacido
y, sin embargo, ha de morir.

Así las cosas, ¿de qué perdida claridad venimos? ¿Quién puede
recordar la inexistencia? Podría ser más dulce regresar, pero

entramos indecisos en un bosque de espinos. No hay nada más
allá de la última profecía. Hemos soñado que un dios lamía
nuestras manos: nadie verá su máscara divina.

Así las cosas,

la locura es perfecta.

[An animal hidden...]

An animal hidden in twilight watches and half pities me. The spoiled fruit hangs heavily, the body's chambers boil. It's exhausting to pass through this illness full of mirrors. Someone whistles in my heart. I don't know who, but I understand the endless syllable.

Blood streaks my thoughts, I write on black tombstones. I am the strange animal. I recognize myself: licking the eyelids he loves, bearing on his tongue a patrilineal spackle. It's me, no doubt: who sings voicelessly and sits down to consider death but finds, instead, only lamps and flies and the labels on funeral ribbons. Sometimes he shouts into still afternoons.

The invisible is inside the light, but does something burn inside the invisible? Our church is impossibility. In any case, the animal refuses to frazzle in agony.

It snaps awake in me when I sleep. It was never born and yet it's just died.

That being the case, from what lost clarity do we come? Who can remember *before* being? It might be sweeter, even, to return, but

we wander indecisively through a forest of thorns. There's nothing beyond the last prophecy. We dreamed a god licked our hands: no one will see its divine mask.

That being the case,

madness is perfect.

Olvido García Valdés

Born in Santianes de Pravia, Asturias, in 1950, she received degrees in Romantic Philology from the University of Oviedo and in Philosophy from the University of Valladolid. Now a Professor of Spanish Language and Literature, she has also directed the Institute Cervantes in Toulouse.

She has published a number of books of poems: *El tercer jardín* (1986), *Exposición* (1990, Premio Ícaro de Literatura), *ella, los pájaros,* (1994, Premio Leonor de Poesía), *caza nocturna* (1997) – translated into Swedish by Ulf Eriksson and into French by Stéphane Chaumet–, *Del ojo al hueso* (2001), *La poesía, ese cuerpo extraño* (Antología) (2005), *Y todos estábamos vivos* (2006) y el libro-disco *El mundo es un jardín* (2010). An anthology of her work, *Racines d'ombre,* has been translated into French by Jean Yves Bériou and Martine Joulia and published in 2010. *Poesía reunida (1982–2008)* brings together her collected poems.

García Valdés is also the author of a biographical essay *Teresa de Jesús* (2001), of texts for art catalogues (on Zush, Kiefer, Tàpies, Broto, and others), and of numerous other literary essays. She has translated books by Pier Paolo Pasolini and co-edited an anthology on Anna Akhmatova and Marina Tsvetaeva. She co-edited the magazines *Los Infolios* (1987–2005) and *El signo del gorrión* (1992–2002). She served as a member of the permanent commision of the Hispanic-Portuguese magazine *Hablar/Falar de poesia* (1996–2002). In 2007 she was awarded the National Poetry Prize.

(De *El tercer jardín,* 1986)

Otro país, otro paisaje,
otra ciudad.
Un lugar desconocido
y un cuerpo desconocido,
tu propio cuerpo, extraño
camino que conduce
directamente al miedo.
El cuerpo como otro,
y otro paisaje, otra ciudad;
atardecer ante las piedras
más dulcemente hermosas
que has visto,
piedras de miel como luz.

Another country, another landscape,
another city.
An unknown place
and an unknown body,
your own body, strange
road leading
straight into dread.
The body as another,
and another landscape, another city;
an evening falling over stones
more tenderly gorgeous
than any you've seen before,
stones of honey like light.

Recordar este sábado:
las tumbas excavadas en la roca,
en semicírculos, mirando
hacia el este,
y la puerta de la muralla abierta
a campos roturados, al silencio
y la luz del oeste. Necesito
los ojos de los lobos
para ver. O el amor y su contacto
extremo, ese filo,
una intimidad sólo formulable
con distancia, con una despiedad
cargada de cuidado.
Así, aquella nota, reconocer en ella
la costumbre antropófaga, un hombre come
una mujer, reconocer
también la carne en carne
viva, los ojos y su atención extrema,
el tiempo y lo que ocurrió.
Alguien lo dijo de otro modo: creí
que éramos infelices muchas veces; ahora

from *Night Hunt*

Remember this Saturday:
tombs excavated from rock,
in semicircles,
facing east,
and the gate in the wall open
to broken fields, to silence
and western light. I need
the eyes of wolves
to see. Or love with its radical
contact, that edge,
an intimacy measured only
in distance, its want of pity
charged with tenderness.
So, on that note, acknowledging
the cannibalistic custom, a man eats
a woman, acknowledging
that flesh lives
on flesh, on eyes and their acute attentiveness,
on the time and what took place.
Someone put it elsewise: many times
I thought we were unhappy; now

la miseria parece que era sólo un aspecto
de nuestra felicidad. La dicha
no eleva sino cae
como una lluvia mansa. Recordar
aquel sábado en febrero
tan semejante a éste de noviembre.
Cerrar los ojos. Fatigarse subiendo,
tú sin voz,
con un cuaderno en el que anotas
lo que quieres decir.
La no materialidad de las palabras
nos da calor y extrañeza, mano
que aprieta el hombro,
aliento cálido sobre el jersey.
Para el resecamiento un aljibe de agua,
los ojos de los lobos
para ver. El contexto
es todo, transparente
aire frío. Aproximadamente así:
campesinos del Tíbet
sentados en el suelo, en semicírculos,
aprendiendo a leer al final del invierno,
cuando el trabajo es poco, se trata
de una foto reciente, están

that misery seems to have been only a face
of our happiness. Bliss
doesn't rise but falls
like softest rain. Remember
that Saturday in February
so like this one in November.
Close your eyes. Wear yourself out
climbing on, you without your voice,
carrying that notebook in which you write
things you'd like to say.
The non-materiality of words
blasts us with heat and surprise, a hand
squeezing a shoulder,
warm breath on a sweater.
To the parched, a jug of water,
the eyes of wolves
to see. Context
is everything, cold
transparent air. Something like this:
Tibetan farmers
sitting on the ground, in semicircles,
learning to read at winter's end,
when work is done, they're discussing
a photograph, they're

muy abrigados; o una paliza
de una violencia extrema
a un muchacho, y que el tiempo
pase, que cure, como una foto antigua.
Tres mariposas, a la luz de la lámpara,
han venido al cristal.

wrapped up warmly; or a boy
beaten to a pulp,
who time leaves behind,
who is restored, like some old photograph.
Three moths, at the lamp's light,
enter the glass.

de *ella, los pájaros,*

te busco por calles
de casas en ruinas y olor acre,
no hay timbres ni nombres;
te encuentro y me miras
pequeño y envejecido, no eres tú,
te pones un sombrero rayado
de ala vuelta y mínima, te vas

I search for you in streets
of wrecked houses and reek,
no bells, no names;
find you and you look at me
small and aging, you not yourself,
adjusting your hat
with its thin band, going off

Tras el cristal, se desconoce
el cuerpo, como un hijo
que crece, como si jugara
y de pronto fuera desconocido.
Coloca entonces
tu mano en el estómago,
la palma abierta, y respira
profundo. Al fin somos culpables
de quien muere, y también
de vivir. Barrios
se hacen poblados peligrosos
por la noche, hay humaredas,
rostros cetrinos junto a fuegos.

Behind the glass, the body is
unknown, like a growing
child, like someone who is fooling
around and then unrecognizable.
So put your
hand on your stomach,
palm open, and breathe
deeply. Finally, we're responsible
for who dies, and also
for who lives. Barrios
are dangerous places
at night, there are smoking barrels,
citrine faces fixed on the fire.

Verde. Las hojas de geranio
en la luz gris de la tormenta
tiemblan, tensión
de nervadura verde oscuro.
Te mirabas las manos,
nervadura de venas; si los dedos
fueran deliciosos, decías.
Al caminar
apoyaba mi sien contra la tuya
y en la noche escuchaba
el ruiseñor y el graznido
del pavo. Indiferencia
de todo, oscuridad.
Me llamabas con voz muy baja.
Sólo un día reíste.

Green. Geranium leaves
in the gray storm light
tremble, a tightening
in the green-dark nervation.
You were looking at your hands,
the nervation of veins; if fingers
were delicious, you were saying.
Walking,
my temple resting against yours
and at night listening
to a nightingale and shrieks
of turkeys. Unconcerned
with anything, blackness.
You were calling me in a low voice.
There was one day you laughed.

Poema Instancias Subjuntivas (III)

Transmuta en campos y hermosura
lo que no se expresa, mira
las mieses, nota el viento, siente
la luz, respira la médula
del mundo, rehaz lo podre
en enjambre y avanza, escucha
su zumbido, toma miel. Di
nombres compañeros, invoca
compañeras. No cejes. Girasoles
y cuervos velan tu corazón. Ablanda
el entrecejo, nutre lo magro. Dispón
vigas de cedro y tablazones
de haya, apacienta entre lirios, mas no olvides
que ira hay en la sabiduría, resplandor
de candela. Llama, di
al viento: ven viento, limpia
esos cielos. Reposa en él los ojos.

Subjective Instances *(III)*

Transmute into fields and loveliness
what you can't express, consider
the crops, note the wind, absorb
the light, sop up the pure marrow
of the world, transform the putrid offering
into a swarm of bees and keep going, listen
for the buzzing, taste the honey. Give
your friends names, invoke
soulmates. Don't quit. Sunflowers
and crows stand watch over your heart. Smooth
out your brow, plump up a little. Set out
cedar beams and beech
planks, graze in the lilies, but don't forget
the rage that comes with knowing, the radiance
in a candle. Call out, say
to the wind: come wind, prepare
the skies. Let your eyes rise there.

Al salir a la calle, sobre los plátanos,
muy por encima y por detrás de sus hojas
doradas y crujientes, el cielo, muy por encima
azul, intenso y transparente de la helada.
A cuatro bajo cero se respira
el aire como si fuera el cielo
que es el aire lo que se respirara.
Corta y se expande y un instante
rebrota antes de herir. Ritmos
de la respiración y el cielo, uno
lugar del otro, volumen
que quien respira retrajera, puro
estar del mundo en el frío,
de un color azul que nadie viera, intenso,
que nadie desde ningún lugar mirara,
aire o cielo no para respirar.

Going out into the street lined with banana trees,
high above and behind their sharp
golden leaves, the sky, blue high
above, intense and icily transparent.
At four below zero, you breathe
air as if it were the sky
you'll come to breathe.
It bites and expands and a moment
blooms before the wounding. Rhythms
of respiration and the sky, one
place among others, a volume
that anyone who breathes-in gives back, pure
presence of the world in the cold,
and a blueness no one can see, so intense
that no one from anywhere will find it,
an air or sky beyond breathing.

de *Y todos estábamos vivos,*

con la luna de marzo llegó
la foto y todos
estábamos vivos;
palabras
de velocidad,
de esa sustancia
que es veloz
y gira y se desprende;
lenta, la luna,
vuelve mes a mes

with March's moon came
the photo and we were all
still alive;
words
that were fleeting,
caught on speed
itself, hurtling and upending;
slowly, the moon,
reappearing month after month

La respuesta era no, para lo más
leve la respuesta era no; no había,
así que no podía ser. Movimientos
debían ceñirse o envararse
como correlato de un también
excluido gasto moral; dispendio
o libertad valoraban leyes
de economía coextensa. Un único
excedente, la ira, arrebatado
impulso que recorría campos y
encendía la casa. Economía
de venas, de piel que busca tacto
y halla aire.

The answer was no, put most
lightly the answer was no; it wasn't,
so it couldn't be. Movements
restrict you or they numb you down
as a correlate of some
disavowed moral expense; debt
or freedom sustain the laws
of a coextensive economy. A unique
surplus, ire, an enraptured
impulse charging through the field and
lighting up the house. An economy
of veins, of skin aching for touch
and meeting with air.

Entre lo literal de lo que ve
y escucha, y otro lugar no evidente
abre su ojo la inquietud. Al lado,
mano pálida de quien convive
con la muerte, cráneo hirsuto. Atendemos
a la oquedad, máscaras que una boca
elabora; distanciada y carnal,
mueve el discurso, lo expande
y desordena, lo concentra, lo apacienta
o dispersa como el lobo a sus corderos.
El sonido de un gong. Es literal
la muerte y las palabras, las bromas
luego de hombres solos, broma y risa
literal. Todo sentido visible, todo
lo visible produce y niega su sentido.
Si respiras en la madrugada, si ves
cómo vuelven imágenes, contémplalas
venir, apaciéntalas, deja que estalle
la inquietud como corderos.

Between the literal of what you see
and hear, and somewhere else not clear,
a disquiet opens your eye. Off to the side,
the pale hand of she who lives
with death, a hirsute skull. We consider
the hollowness, the masks that a mouth
marks out; distanced and carnal,
discourse moves on, it expands
and breaks up, it concentrates, it grazes
or scatters like lambs before a wolf.
The sound of a gong. It is literal,
death, and the words, the jibes following
single men, joking and the literal
laughing. All visible sense, all that is
visible produces and denies its meaning.
If you breathe in the morning, if you notice
how images return, consider their
coming, graze on them, let the disquiet
explode like lambs.

Vamos cayendo como moscas,
tener presente, de duelo y compañía,
esa expresión: Pilar, Esther,
Lucía, Teresa, Concha o
Lola, Ángeles, Lourdes. No saber bien
si se vive. Entre pararse y hacer
sin descanso, alucinada la diferencia
es de concentración o de ortopedia.
Dejarse ir o remar un poco más
contra corriente, no hacer pausas.

                                        Sólo,

de pronto, tiemblan las hierbas junto a
los rosales, el césped que habría
ya que haber segado, la brisa lo hace
brillar, movilidad de cada brizna, zig
zag, latiguillo en el hueso de la ceja.

We go on falling like flies,
bearing in mind, with regard to grief and company,
that expression: Pilar, Esther,
Lucia, Teresa, Concha or
Lola, Angel, Lourdes. Not really knowing
if you're alive. Between stopping and restlessly
working, deluded, the difference
is a matter of concentration or orthopedics.
Letting go or paddling a little further
upstream, without taking a rest.

                                            Only,

suddenly, the weeds tremble against
the rose bushes, the grass that should already
have been cut, the wind makes it
shine, eloquence of each blade, zig
zag, bend of eyebrow on bone.

Juntas en la cocina sin apenas
hablar, un lugar no exclusivo
de mujeres, que sigue al parecer siendo
exclusivo. Casi nada en común,
salvo contradicciones que sujetan
y asemejan, nos enmarca este espacio
al que creemos ya no pertenecer. De ellos
el mundo y la sala grande, conversación
de lengua reductora, el chiste sexual,
la perspectiva hollada, cierto
poder, risas, el mundo. Al mundo
salgo que es único consuelo, campos
y árboles hoy que es mayo, y la savia
estalla verde y varón según la lengua,
el mundo que consuela y el que no,
ajenos ambos hoy a mí, que camino
con daño en lo ajeno que la vida deja.

from *And We Were All Still Alive*

Together in the kitchen barely
speaking, a place not exclusive
to women though it continues to seem
exclusive. Almost nothing in common
but contradictions bind
and liken us, we're framed in spaces
we don't think we belong to. Of these,
the world and the living room, conversation
in a reductive language, sexual puns,
a flattened perspective, the whiff
of power, laughter, the world. The world
I take to be a singular consolation, fields
and trees, today it's May and the sap
runs murky and masculine through our language,
the world that comforts and that doesn't,
both alien to me now as I walk with my
wounds in the oblivion life begrudges me.

ganar un día cada día, llegar
a la noche y respirar, con cada movimiento
ir haciendo, del ritmo de la respiración,
aliento para llegar
al día

from *And We Were All Still Alive*

to win the day every day, to come into
the night breathing, to be doing something
with every gesture, in respiration's rhythm,
provision for meeting
the day

Miguel Casado

Miguel Casado (Valladolid, 1954) is the author of many books of poetry, criticism, and translation. In poetry, his books include *Inventario* (Premio Hiperión, 1987), *Falso movimiento, La mujer automática* y *Tienda de fieltro*. His critical writing has been collected in *Del caminar sobre hielo, La poesía como pensamiento, Los artículos de la polémica y otros textos sobre poesía, Deseo de realidad, El curso de la edad: Lecturas de Antonio Gamoneda o La experiencia de lo extranjero*. The most recent book of essays is *La palabra sabe*. Casado's translations include *La soñadora materia* by Francis Ponge y the *Obra poética* of Arthur Rimbaud.

En la ciudad

Ocurre a veces este retorno
de los jóvenes fascistas, esas pintadas,
los símbolos. Algunos
bromean, es posible
que otros estén asustados,
circulan en coche, no les importa
dejar manchas en los asientos.
La pared distribuye, alrededor
de sus letras
negras y torcidas, anuncios
de pocos colores. Bromean, sí,
se divierten. Con pasquines
pequeños tapan escaparates
de comercios en quiebra.

In the City

It happens now and again, this return
of the young fascists, that graffiti,
the symbols. Some
laugh it off, it's likely
others are spooked,
driving aimlessly, not noticing
they've left stains on the seats.
Parceled out among
the black and twisted
letters on the wall
are duotone ads. They're joking, sure,
they're screwing around. With
placards they
plug the windows
of bankrupt businesses.

***

Encerrado, anota sin pausa,
se pregunta obsesivamente
por cómo se percibe, cómo se nombra
lo que se percibe, sobre todo
los colores - "en la paleta, el blanco
es el color más claro", o por qué
"algo transparente
puede ser verde, pero nunca blanco"-.
Escribe a mano, luego dicta
a máquina; recorta trozos
de papel y los separa, pega unos
en otros, no recuerda lo escrito
antes y, en el desorden de la memoria,
encuentra palabras libres
que pesan, destellos, líneas
que el pensamiento
aún recorre.

***

Shut in, writing without pause,
he obsessively wonders
how we perceive things, how names
are given to them, especially
the colors – "on the palette white
is the lightest color," and why
"something can be transparent green
but not transparent white –".
Later, writing by hand, he dictates
to the machine; he clips pieces
of paper, spreads them out, pastes
some over others, can't remember what
he wrote earlier and, in memory's disorder,
weighs stray words,
flashes, lines
that thought
jams together.

Entre Belmonte y Madrigal

Extramuros es una estepa rasa
donde las paredes van perfilando
su curva arenosa y mordida,
lo que serán ladrillos sueltos,
arcos ciegos. La torre
en la esquina, más alta.
Extramuros es la mancha
sin nombre de todo radio,
la extrema visibilidad,
los círculos frenéticos en vuelo,
los montículos, los trozos rojos
dispersos a la mano.

El ritmo del caminante
varía: la punta doblada
de las pajas, los revoloteos
y ruidos, la pérdida hacia dentro
en un tiempo oscuro.
De puerta a puerta,
alfileres de polvo,
bocanada ardiente.

Between Belmonte and Madrigal

Extramuros is a broad steppe
where the convent's walls still stand, profiling
a sandy, pocked curvature,
what will come to be scattered bricks,
blind arches. The corner
tower higher yet.
Extramuros is the unnamed
stain of pure radium,
hyper-visibility,
the wild loops of swifts in the air,
mounds, red fragments
collected by hand.

The walker's pace
varies: the bent tips
of wheat, fluttering
and noise, an inward-directed loss
in a dark time.
From door to door,
needles of dust,
burning mouthfuls.

Existen lugares de la meditación,
lugares de la vida, se agotan
estos lugares. Ver y no ver
en el camino, oír y no oír
en los encuentros. Se agotan
y el que permanece
en el monólogo aquel de la mojama
inscribe su muesca.
De un cerro a otro
se adapta la muralla
a las ondulaciones, encierra
olivos, toma cipreses.

O el hundimiento
donde se conservan vigas,
donde la solidez de las piedras
envuelve. Patio triangular,
ventanas como huecos últimos
a donde accede el gozo.
Estrellas de trigo.

There are places of meditation,
places rammed with life, and these places
are wiped away. Seeing and not seeing
along the road, in brief encounters, hearing
and not hearing. They're wiped away
and he who dwells
in that monologue of the salted fish
may yet make his mark.
From one hill to another
the wall pursues
undulations, enclosing
olive trees, claiming cypresses.

Or the hollow
where joists remain,
where the surround is a solidity
of stone. A triangular patio,
windows, the last vents
giving access to joy.
Stars of wheat.

Notas sobre el antiguo tema de dejar la ciudad

A medida que se renuevan las calles
y que caduca su costumbre,
de la ciudad van quedando sólo
los fantasmas. Versátiles en las esquinas,
como un código de signos que no se acusa
en los ojos, sensaciones del estómago,
opacas en la frente interior.
Algunos que desean saber, no preguntan
por la niñez de los padres. Un mendigo
de barba blanca hurga en la papelera,
luego se aleja sin acercarse a pedir.

Notes on the Old Theme of Leaving the City

As they repave the streets
and the familiar expires,
only ghosts go on, sticking it out
in the city. On the corners, they're versatile
as a code of signs that doesn't register
in the eyes, sensations in the stomach,
opaque against the brow's interior.
Some want to know but don't inquire
about their parents' childhoods. A white-
bearded beggar pokes through the bin
then drifts off without bothering to ask.

***

La rama en el ojo,
como en el árbol, desnuda,
que el viento bambolea.
Sube y baja con el viento,
azota, misteriosamente
se la ve desde un sótano,
al pie de una escalera.

***

A branch in the eye
matches the one in the tree, so bare
the wind staggers there.
Rising and falling in wind, see –
it thrashes, enigmatically
glimpsed from a basement
at the foot of the stairs.

***

Ahora que la cabeza está llena
de una pasta esponjosa
y continua, en que nada
toma luz, se mira las manos
y encuentra el extraño callo de escritor:
hendido y rojo un momento
por la presión de la pluma. Y lee
sin entender la grafía negra,
esa forma plana del deseo,
plana y estéril.

***

Now that the head is full
of a spongy, endless
paste in which nothing
lights up, he notices his hands
and finds the writer's curious callus:
cracked and red for a moment
by the pen's pressure. And reads
without understanding the black script,
that flattened form of desire,
flat and sterile.

***

La madre urge a la niña, le dice
que su hermano, al que lleva en brazos
-con más de treinta meses le cuelga doblada
la cabeza-, pesa como un muerto.
Y las palabras resbalan por el cuerpo dormido
y caen al suelo entra las dos;
la niña mira, con cuidado de no pisarlas.

***

The mother implores the girl, complaining
that her brother, whom she holds in her arms
–at more than thirty months, his head still
droops–, is like a dead weight.
And the words slide over that sleeping body
and fall to the floor between them;
the girl glances down, careful not to squash them.

***

Esta ciudad te ha conducido
al extrarradio, a un laberinto de aceras
y miradas donde tu monodia
no se interrumpe. Ahora que debo
inventar tus emociones, parece
que yo estuviera lleno de ellas.
Arrastras los pies y te digo: ten
paciencia, no podemos hacer nada;
sólo esa palabra, *malita,* repites
una vez. De tan claros, los ojos
se han quedado fijos, y busco
también en el espejo sus legañas, bolitas
de gelatina azul, las gotas que escurren
por los pelillos. Siguen el golpe
del agua mis dedos en tu garganta,
y vuelves con silencio a preguntar,
a temblar en tu conocimiento
incomprensible.

***

This city has brought you
to the outskirts, a maze of sidewalks
and glances where your monody
goes uninterrupted. Now that I have to
invent your emotions, it appears
I was loaded with them.
You shuffle your feet and I tell you: be
patient, we can't do anything;
there are two words, *poor thing*, you repeat
once. Eyes can fix
on such clarities, and I'm examining
their bleariness in the mirror, blue-
jellied marbles, drops squeezed out
over the tiny hairs. My fingers massage
the gulp of water down your throat,
and you return in silence to wonder,
to tremble in your incomprehensible
knowing.

***

Hace ya muchos años, quizá
treinta, que puedo contar estas historias
de otro mundo: caminos
entre huertas, montículos junto al tren,
barrios todavía de trazado
medieval. Ha sido una tarea
minuciosa de destrucción, terminó
hace ya muchos años. Ahora
algunos viernes duermo en un hotel,
me siento a comer en las terrazas
de la calle, donde ponen
un café de puchero; apenas conozco
ciertos códigos de la costumbre, cada vez
menos, y me extrañan los nombres
que leo en la prensa. Es bueno estar lejos
los que fuimos testigos.

***

For many years now, maybe
thirty, I've been telling these stories
of another world: lanes
through orchards, trains skirting hilltops,
neighborhoods still almost
medieval. It was a meticulous
labor of destruction which ended
many years ago. Now,
I sometimes sleep in hotels on Friday,
I sit down to eat on street terraces
where they plop down
a coffee pot; I can barely recall
the basic social codes, each time
fewer, and I miss the names
I read in the papers. It's better to keep our distance,
we who were witnesses.

***

Ella leía poemas
de rara intensidad, concentrada
dijo que no había visto
las golondrinas. De lo que pensé
mientras una leía y otras volaban
−naturaleza, arte, disonancia
y armonía− sólo queda una duda
sobre la interpretación. Sublime
todo y grotesco, el vuelo ágil
angosto, esbelto y glotón entre los mosquitos,
la música chirriante, no puede
deslindarse de una duda
sobre la falta de fin, también
sobre la imposible esperanza.

***

She read poems
of a remarkable intensity; wholly engrossed,
she said she hadn't noticed
the swallows. Of whatever I thought
while one read and others flew
−nature, art, dissonance
and harmony−all that remains unclear
is the interpretation. Everything
sublime and grotesque, the gracile narrow
flight, lissome and gluttonous among mosquitoes,
the squeaky music. No one
can distance themselves from doubt
about the lack of an ending or about
irremediable hope.

Marcos Canteli

Marcos Canteli was born in Bimenes, Asturias, Spain in 1974. He received his B.A. from the University of Oviedo, and his Ph.D. from Duke University. He works as Resident Director for Duke University in Madrid. He has published four books of poetry: *Reunión* (Barcelona: Icaria, 1999), *enjambre* (Madrid: Bartleby, 2003), *su sombrío* (Barcelona: DVD, 2005, XXXI Ciudad de Burgos International Poetry Award), and *catálogo de incesantes* (Madrid: Bartleby, 2008), and *es brizna* (Valencia: Editorial Pre-Textos, 2010). He translated Robert Creeley's *Pieces [Pedazos]* (Madrid: Bartleby, 2005), and Jack Kerouac's *Book of Haikus [Libro de jaikus]* (Madrid: Bartleby, 2007). He is the editor of http://www.7de7.net (revista de escritura & poéticas) and of dandolavoz.blogspot.com.

ììì

lo que no poseemos
va a durar

la bañera sobre la hierba el abrevadero al fondo
moho de los ojos la depresión musical
que no existe

ni tus pétalos abiertos pero en otro mundo sí

la lamina que escribo
en la disolución

y que al volver a casa la casa ya no está

from *Breathblade*

iii

what we don't own
will last

the little bath on the grass the trough at its bottom
eye – mold a musical slump
that doesn't exist

nor do your petals open but in another world

I write a lamina
over the dissolution

and upon returning to the house the house isn't there

ììì

la casa la casa que esencialmente no tenemos

los ojos claros su propio aislante me dicen
muere el canto el ojo aquí de mañana

aquel parche pájaros maderas crujientes aquí

no era ni es vestigio porque viene
largos de agua árboles escritos a su calor

iii

the house the house that most essentially we don't own

the brightness of the eyes their own insulation suggests
the song dies the eye here starting tomorrow

that patch creaky wooden birds here

it wasn't nor is it a vestige since it derives
at long watery last from heatwritten trees

ììì

y esta aleación de flujo y pena

a los traductores invisibles desde la cerradura
a la Virgen que lamió el cerebro de mamá

en el jaiku en la sicodelia del jaiku mi tiritar
renovable de verano

nada es estanco a nada

ììì

and this alloy of flux and shame

to the invisible translators from the closing
to the Virgin who licked her mother's brain

in the haiku in the psychedelia of haiku my renewable
shivering in summer

nothing is impervious to anything

ììì

cereza despacio / qué silenciosa / lamía su escarcha

su cerebro renegrido / mi mamá / me mira

de las dos ramas de albahaca / una enferma / mis dos ojos

iii

Slow cherry / so silent / licking at the frost

brain blackened / my mother / stares at me

one of two branches of basil / sickens both / of my eyes

ìì

hoy la fascinación
es metálica precisa la mente cayó en pena
flexible tu vena de ley trabaja con tu ley

la luna del murmullo es tú es una cruz el nudo
deshacer ese nudo para volverte preciso

hoy los árboles son árboles sentarse
no es detenerse sino reconocer
un fluido

ese frío nos hace más hospitalarios la médula lo mide
una excelente lesión que no pasó factura

ììì

today's fascination
is necessarily metallic the mind goes down in pain
your ductile vein of law works with your law

the moon of murmurs is you yourself are a cross knot
undo that knot to return to your necessary self

today the trees are trees sitting down
is less a pause than a recognition of
fluency

the cold makes us more hospitable the medulla measures out
an excellent lesion that has yet to take its toll

resuena como un proverbio

pensar en la renuncia a la clausura ⊠ deja perder (cuestion de
carácter) la vista este ermitaño y por el cráter de su herida pasta
un ahora / japonesa ansia, de un vacío *all-inclusive,*

        como un reguero de voladores

    al resplandor de tus uñas   diseccionar

    en amistad de animales

    por autopistas este país

               a cántaros

ser claros ⊠ desorden de día de brotes / y no hay insectos en
el relente (aunque no se pueda ya decir así) ⊠ es renuncia la
clausura

reverberating like a proverb

considering the renunciation of the clause ☒ he allows (a
question of character) his sight to fail this hermit and on his
cratered contusion a now / japanese anxiety grazes, from an
all-inclusive void,

> like a dribble of fireworks
> the glow of your fingernails   might dissect
> in animal camaraderie
> this country by its byways

                                        by the bucketsful
to be clear cut ☒ disarray of the budding day / and not a
single insect in the drizzle (although you can't quite yet say) ☒
the renunciation is a clause

entonces: epitafios

del ojo contra un sentido común en trincheras / de cuanto viene
de atrás en borrasca ☒ manzana de dolor
                                 gato de dolor
              en lengua
              como del sueño aquella
                                 pista de tenis
              inglés de
              Canterbury Birchington Sarre Ct.
              primer menstruo
              que fue perceptción de limite
                                              y
casi mística
paráfrasis de ahora ☒ probable aparición de agua dura
por fatiga del material ☒ mis venas, que en desvergüenza
enraízan (radicalizan) al corte cada vez más la mano ☒
Richter: el arte es la más alta forma de esperanza / y si médula,
siempre de una masturbación amarga ☒ del cuarto oscuro salí
con deseo sólo de pelaje

then: epitaphs

from the eye against a feeling common to the trenches / of
whatever comes after as storm ☒ apple of pain
                          cat of pain
                in a dream-
                like language that

                                    English tennis
                court at
                Canterbury Birchington Sarre Ct.
                first menstruation
                as a glimpse of the end

                                                            and

almost mystical
gloss on the now ☒ it's likely the water's apparition endures
beyond the fatigue of material ☒ my shameless veins which
take root (radicalize) deeper in the cut each time the hand ☒
so Richter: *art is the highest form of hope* / without hope, which
sometimes grows on trees ☒ epitaphs, but whose / and if
marrow, always from an agonizing masturbation ☒ all I felt
leaving the dark room was the longing for such a pelt

combine

es acuático / entra y crece ese árbol por la puerta, nada en
libertad, mira siempre más allá de lo que rodea ☒ tarjas
estelas estatuas

rituales señuelos

y

ardides ☒ a lo que viene sólo en membranas ☒ pan al
hueso / y un arte entonces de retales y nada romántico, un
aislamiento en favor de la situación volátil ☒ llamarla propia
porque adamada se extiende ☒ retribuciones que son casi
escarnios, amor que sin ojos crece ☒ transferirse en sueño,
permeable al sentido de lugar, desclavarse de la camisa de
fuerza / bien por las ramas o caminos complejos al ojo ☒ del
mundo,

y el cabello verde
el cabello rosa
su fluido

combine

aquatic, it / shows up and grows a tree by the door, no longer
free to go, always searching the beyond that surrounds it ☒
rods

             obelisks statues

                    ritual marks

             and

schemes ☒ regarding what only comes wrapped in membrane
☒ bread to the bone / and an art then of pieces and *nothing
romantic,* isolation chosen over volatile situation ☒ calling it
by name elegant because it expands ☒ retributions that are
all but humiliations, love that grows blind ☒ passed along in
dream, sensitive to a sense of place, pulling free of the straight
jacket / whether on branches or roads that look complicated to
the eye ☒ of the world,

             and the green hair
             the red hair
             streaming

acercándose: el espejo

importante es volar
a raíz de agua
                atrás
agua atrás
porque aunque queridas o no, razones hubo para el éxodo ⊠ y
de
aquella niñez de monedas que eran añicos mutaciones de la
casa, su vaho, el de un vaso rápido, lenta memoria ⊠ cruje la
nieve, mi escopeta de perdigones la que escondiste, mi mirilla
igual, chascan ⊠ en esta realidad luz de color, no hay miedo,
sino hongo de nieve historia ⊠ porque un poeta tiene que
revolver, porque tal vez no hace cuarenta sino treinta y dos años
nací en una mesa, pero entretelas y si no allí
                ¿dónde?
reflejándose ⊠ a contracorriente de ramas, un viento en el
menaje, senderos ⊠ por más que podre y viéndola arder, raíz
siempre ⊠ suelta esa mano,
                unas alas
                    abren poda
entre maleza

approaching: the mirror

it's important to fly
to the source of water
                    going back
backwater
because like it or not, there are reasons for the exodus ☒ and
out of that childhood of coins, the shattered mutations of the
house, its gas, lifting quickly from a glass, memory, in slow-
mo, ☒ crosses the snow, my shotgun of buckshot which you
hid with my scope, they click ☒ in this lifelike glow of light,
there's no fear, only the shroom of historical snow ☒ because
a poet has to return, because maybe it's not forty but thirty two
years ago I was born on a table, so go ahead, enter into them
and if not there
                    where then?
finding itself deflected ☒ across the branches, a wind through
the house, paths ☒ through worse than pus and watching it
burn, the source always ☒ soothes the hand,
                    the wings
                              opening to prune
the underbrush

que ya no

ya no hay cántaros ni jofainas aguamaniles, artos brezos, hartos,
arras son obsenas que no deberíamos ver ☒ mi madre dice su
artritis mi padre su alergia, yo el plexo oscuro, la rama nerviosa
que es red, o la progresiva ceguera de mi animal ☒ palidecen
ante los ojos los meros ojos ☒ mi animal de aprendizaje,
entre el desarraigo memoria por sendero, y ahí sí, un amago
de pasadizo, en la escritura una hemorragia de luz ☒ como ir
tierno al pulmón del día, pero qué loza lavará ese día

already not here

now there are neither pitchers basins nor jugs, heather
hedges, plenty, and what we pledge is too obscene to be seen
☒ my mother says her arthritis my father his allergy, me my
dark plexus, the nerve branch of the network, my animal's
progressive blindness ☒ paling before my eyes my very eyes
☒ my apprentice animal, lost among memory's deracinated
paths, until there it is, a hint of a passage, in the scribble a
hemorrhage of light ☒ like the lung of day turning tender, but
how will it wash out and in what crockery

Sandra Santana

Sandra Santana was born in Madrid in 1978. She has a Ph.D. in Philosophy from the Universidad Complutense in Madrid and she completed postgraduate studies at the University of Viena and the University of Humboldt in Berlin. She received a creative fellowship from the Madrid Arts Foundation for Students in 2002–2004. Her books of poems include *Marcha por el desierto* and *Es el verbo tan frágil* (Pre-Textos, 2008) as well as the essay collection *El laberinto de la palabra, Karl Kraus y la cuestión lingüística en la Viena fin de siglo* (Acantilado, 2011). As a translator, she has published versions of Karl Kraus, Ernst Jandl and Peter Handke. She is a member of the experimental literary group El águila ediciones.

*   *   *

El médico le rogó que tratase de ser más concisa: "Exactamente, ¿dónde le duele?". Pero, en el transcurso del movimiento del dedo índice hacia la rodilla, aquel dolor metálico se disolvía en una especie de cosquilleo burbujeante en el talón izquierdo. Detuvo la mano avergonzada y empezó de nuevo, tratando esta vez de prestar un poco más de atención.

*   *   *

The doctor asked her to try to be more concise: "Exactly where does it hurt?" But even as her index finger approached her knee, the metallic pain dissolved into a kind of fizzy tingling in her left heel. Embarrassed, she paused and began again, this time trying to pay stricter attention.

De la carestía del argumento o qué se hizo de lo inenarrable

El tema es desde luego intratable.

No fue lo que dijimos,
no fue lo que dejamos por decir, tampoco
desembocó en una decisión.

Apenas se lastimó nuestro tejido
argumental dejando un espacio
abierto para lo porvenir.

On the Cost of the Argument or What Became of the Unspeakable

The theme is indeed intractable.

It wasn't what we said,
it wasn't what we left unsaid, neither
led to a decision.

It just ruptured our argumental
fabric, leaving an open
space for what might come.

Asuntos acerca de los cuales lamento no tener una
brillante opinión que dar a los lectores

Con la llegada de la noche
algunas de sus palabras, como el arder
intermitente [Aquí, detecté un punto
de inflexión provocado por la extraña
naturaleza del deseo.

Comprendí que
más rápido que la imaginación,
puesto que no necesita movimiento,
espera siempre oculto
en todos los lugares] de un cigarro,
llamaban un instante luminoso
mi atención antes de consumirse.

*Matters About Which Unfortunately I Have No Brilliant
Opinion to Offer Readers*

With the arrival of the night
some of his words, like the intermittent
flare [Here, I detected a point
of inflection provoked by the peculiar
nature of desire.

Which came to me
even faster than imagination
since it needs not move at all,
waiting hidden always
everywhere] of a cigarette,
called my attention to a luminous
moment before it faded away.

*   *   *

Provocar un cambio en aquella situación, una variación en
los acontecimientos, se había vuelto más fácil que impedirlo.
Consciente de este hecho, su voz avanzaba sigilosamente en
las conversaciones que con él mantenía. Cualquier giro brusco,
cualquier crujido en el espacio intervocálico o una interjección
pronunciada sin el suficiente cuidado podía hacerse inopinada-
mente con las riendas de su destino.

*   *   *

Forcing a change in the situation, a variation on events, became easier than stopping them altogether. Aware of this fact, she released her voice stealthily into their conversations. Any sharp turn, any crack in the intervocalic space or an interjection tendered without sufficient caution could unexpectedly yield the reins of her destiny.

Nuevas consideraciones acerca del destino del agua

La tormenta aguardaba
respirando despacio.
De pronto echa a correr y todas las preguntas
caen agotadas
desde la orilla de nuestros labios.

Entiéndeme, vivir es tan difícil, es un verbo tan frágil, tan incon-
stante... En cuanto le pones un dedo encima comienza a vibrar, a
moverse, a perder su forma.

Mi suspicacia hace
que se rompa la tarde
y la superficie del cielo,
como el vidrio por un leve golpe,
descubre una grieta infinita.

Continúa entero, créeme,
incluso más hermoso,
pero exhibiendo ahora
impúdicamente su fragilidad,
su condición de material efímero.

Fresh Considerations on the Fate of Water

The storm brewed
in slow breaths.
Then it comes on fast and all the questions
fall exhausted
from the rims of our lips.

Listen to me, living is hard enough, it's a verb so fragile, so fickle ...
As soon as you put a finger on it, it starts vibrating, shifting, slipping
out of itself.

My suspicions are enough
to shatter the afternoon
and the thin veneer of the sky,
as a pane of glass that, tapped lightly,
lets loose an infinite howl.

The whole thing keeps going, believe me,
it's even more beautiful,
but exhibiting, shamelessly
now, its fragility,
its true status as ephemeral material.

de *Es el verbo tan frágil*

Luces de interior

(Siempre nos dejamos conmover
por la sinceridad
que otros confeccionan
con tanta precisión).

Su calidez
hará que podáis sentir en las paredes
el continuo latir del presente.

No vamos a rendirnos precisamente
cuando tratan de esclarecer
la distancia máxima de seguridad
entre lo posible
y los raudos sueños de la audiencia.

Aplausos

Mejor seguir mirando la pantalla
y apoyar, sobre tu hombro,
mi cabeza.

Interior Lights

(We always allow ourselves be moved
by the sincerity
others so
unerringly concoct).

Its warmth
is such that you can feel in the walls
the ceaseless throb of the present.

We're not going to give up just
when they try to elucidate
the maximum safe distance
between the possible
and the whistling sleep of the audience.

Applause

Better to keep watching the screen
and support, on your shoulder,
my head.

de *Datos*

Efectivamente, la fantasía erótica es el espacio donde
con mayor claridad las rutas del sueño y la vigilia se
muestran como una ancha carretera de doble dirección

Imposible reprimir aquel repentino exceso de sudoración. Su lengua no estaba allí y, sin embargo, sentía con total nitidez una tibia humedad en el cuello.

***

No fue el iris, sino la pupila lo que le hizo perder la concentración. Su fantasía –rápida, rápida– había actuado directamente sobre la realidad y se concentraba en esa parte negra e invariable del ojo a modo de tragaluz. Experimentó una ligera sensación de vértigo al sentir cómo su cuerpo la seguía jadeante, buscando algún punto donde detenerse.

***

Le sedujo aquella manera de mirarle y preguntar cuál era el modo más rápido de llegar al centro. Confiando en la inviolabilidad del pensamiento, le instó a subir juntos las escaleras de casa e improvisaron allí un ejercicio de sincronización perfecta donde tanto una leve presión sobre el muslo como el retorcimiento de un brazo o una brusca sacudida por la espalda era percibido por ambos como el alivio de una urgente necesidad antes desconocida. De regreso a la pregunta: "¿Sabe usted si tardará mucho en pasar el próximo tren en dirección a la estación central?", ella enrojeció y se encogió de hombros.

Actually, Erotic Fantasy is the Space Wherein with Greatest Clarity the Paths of Dream and Wakefulness are Revealed as a Two-lane Highway

Unable to suppress the sudden whelm of sweat. His tongue wasn't there but, nevertheless, she clearly felt the warm moistness at her neck.

***

It wasn't the iris, not the pupil either that instigated the loss of concentration. His fantasy—quickly, quickly—had intensified reality and focused itself like a skylight on the invariable and black dot of her eye. She felt a light vertigo when she realized her body was still panting, searching for a place to stop.

***

He seduced her by staring at her and asking for the quickest way to the center. Relying on the inviolability of thought, she insisted they go up the stairs of the house together to improvise there an exercise in perfect synchronization where even the lightest pressure on her thigh, the twist of an arm or a sudden jolt to her back was perceived both as relief and as an urgency for the as yet unknown. Returning to the question: "Do you have any idea if the next train for central station is late?" she blushed and shrugged.

Naturalis historiae (o lo que el vertebrado más sofisticado tiene en común con un molusco gasterópodo)

Lo peor esperaba tras el fundido en negro de un buen sueño.
Se asustó ante la visión de su propio cuerpo tumbado a solas,
en penumbra, y vio desprenderse entonces del alto techo una
viejísima sonrisa burlona.

***

Las gafas y el pañuelo fueron cuidadosamente escogidos.
Indiferente, con el olor salino de la costa, emerge sin embargo
la carne blanda desde la sombra húmeda de la camisa.

***

Bajo el abrigo, el grito de todos aquellos cuerpos desnudos.
Una visión espantosa, complicada por las costumbres de la
educación, por aquel ir y venir de bolsas.

***

Incontrolable ese continuo coro atravesando la cavidad única
de su boca, aquella gigantesca muestra zoológica apoderándose
secuencialmente de su voz.

from *Data*

Natural History (Or What the Most Sophisticated Vertebrate Shares in Common with a Gastropod Mollusk)

At worst, she waited behind the black burnout of a good sleep. She panicked at the sight of her own body upended and solitary in darkness, and saw sloughing right then from the high ceiling, a primeval sneer.

***

The glasses and handkerchief were carefully chosen. Regardless, with a coastal saline odor, flabby flesh emerges from the damp shadows of her shirt.

***

Under the coat, the cry of all those naked bodies. A terrifying vision, complicated by the conventions of education, by that coming and going with bags.

***

Uncontrollable, a steady chorus cutting through the unique cavity of her mouth, that enormous zoological specimen gradually taking control of her voice.

El horóscopo acierta azarosamente en su pronóstico: "Tu corazón, en cambio, está triste"

El cierre de la velada fue sorprendente. Fuera del coche la luz del atardecer tomó por un momento el matiz de apertura del amanecer. Como si ahora fuera posible salir de allí y marchar hacia atrás sonriendo en la extraña blancura del paisaje. Las señales de prohibición, las extrañas vaquitas de los campos. Dejarse llevar por entusiasmo de la fe, sentir la fuerza del salto inesperado.

***

Consideraba los vagones de metro un espacio a la medida de sus propias fuerzas. Encontrarse en su interior suponía que, por algún motivo, se había levantado de la cama (de aquella blanda inercia) renunciando a que un factor externo (independiente, por tanto, de ella y de su toma de decisiones) viniese inesperadamente en su ayuda. "El vagón por dentro –se dijo– parece un repugnante intestino". Inspiró profundamente y se tranquilizó pensando en la reluciente cáscara de metal que la envolvía.

***

The Horoscope Eventfully Announces Your Prognosis: *"Your Heart, on the Other Hand, Is Sad"*

The evening's end was amazing. Outside the car the falling light took on for a moment hues of the crack of dawn. As if now it were possible to clear out of there and head back smiling into the weird wanness of the landscape. The no trespassing signs, the weird little cows in the fields. Getting carried away with an enthusiasm for faith, feeling the force of the sudden leap.

***

She imagined the subway cars offered a space proportional to her own powers. Finding herself in their interiors, she supposed that, by some means, she'd been raised from the bed (of some dull inertia) denying that there was any external power (independent, then, from her and her decision making) that might unexpectedly come to her rescue. "The interior of the car," she thought, "looks like a filthy intestine." Breathing deeply, she calmed herself by focusing on the the shiny metal that surrounded her.

***

La ventaja de haber preparado antes cuidadosamente todos los elementos de aquella trampa le hacía saber exactamente lo que había que hacer para caer en ella. Una vez estuvo lista, siguió punto por punto sus propias y astutas indicaciones.

***

"En ocasiones –le dijo sin dejar de mirar el nacimiento de las uñas– abrir una ventana no requiere fuerza física, ni habilidad manual. La dificultad reside, sencillamente, en esquivar el miedo a descubrir que el aire que ahora respiras no es suficientemente bueno porque está cargado con su respiración; la posibilidad de que el aire renovado entre con demasiada fuerza, de modo que ya no seas capaz de volver a cerrarla".

***

Gestionaba su miseria con la mayor precaución. Al mostrarla se arriesgaba a que otros la recibieran en un estado anímico distinto del suyo, a que –incluso si la escuchaban con atención– acabase confundida con recuerdos y matices que no le pertenecían. La posibilidad de que se cometiera este abuso con sus sentimientos más íntimos le convertía en víctima de un abatimiento aún más profundo.

The advantage of having earlier carefully prepared all the elements of the trap allowed her to know precisely what to do to fall into it. Once she was ready, she followed point by point the well-scripted directions.

***

"Sometimes," he said without looking away from his emerging fingernails, "opening a window requires neither physical strength nor manual skill. The challenge is simply to suppress the fear that you'll discover the air you're breathing now isn't any good because it's saturated with breathing; the possibility that fresh air would rush in with so much force that you wouldn't be capable of closing the window again."

***

She managed her misery with enormous caution. Whenever she showed up, she took the risk that she would be meeting others whose states of mind were so distinct from her own that–even if they listened to her attentively–they would end up confusing memories with details that were utterly unrelated. The possibility that this abuse was perpetrated by her most intimate feelings subjected her to an even deeper depression.

Benito del Pliego

Benito del Pliego (Madrid, 1970) has published the following poetry books: *Fisiones* (Madrid, 1997); *Alcance de la mano* (New Orleans, 1998); *Índice* (Valencia, 2004, and Madrid, 2011), the plaquette *Zodiaco* (Bogotá, 2007), *Merma* (Tenerife, 2009), *Muesca* (Madrid, 2010), and *Fábula* (Badajoz: Aristas Martínez Ediciones, 2012).

He has also written critical pieces about contemporary Spanish exiled writers in the Americas, and Latin American poets who migrated to Spain within the last few decades. He has translated Isel Rivero's English poetry (*Las palabras son testigos/Words are witnesses* (Madrid, 2010). In collaboration with Andrés Fisher, he has edited José Viñals' anthology *Caballo en el Umbral* (Mérida, 2010); they are currently translating to Spanish a selection of Gertrude Stein's writings. He is associate professor at the Department of Foreign Languages and Literatures at Appalachian State University (in North Carolina). The poems included here are part of an abecedarian.

El burro:

(Christopher Winsor)

—«El que solo ve lo que otros buscan no sabe ver a los que encuentran.

Saber música porque se aprendió no tiene mérito.

Quien hace sonar la caña en el prado por azar, sabe más; sabe de un saber mayor y por sorpresa lo entiende.»

The Ass:

(Christopher Winsor)

– "Those who see only what others look for don't know
how to see what they find.

To know music because what's understood is without merit.

Whoever blows a note from a reed by chance, knows more;
tastes a deeper knowing and, in surprise, comprehends it."

El camaleón:

–«Ni el ser ni el parecer te pertenecen: lo ajeno es lo que te hace y te transforma.

Si miras a fondo, despreocupado del color de los ojos con que miras, lo que ves te libera.

La verdadera pasión, la pasión del instante, adelanta la disolución final, que es camuflaje perpetuo.»

The Chameleon:

– "Neither being nor seeming concern you: it's the foreign that makes and transforms you.

If you glance back, incognizant of the color of the eyes through which you look, what you see frees you.

The real passion, the passion of the moment, brings on the final dissolution, which is continuous camouflage."

El dado:

(Joan Brossa)

–«Apuesto que le preocupa el destino y que el sabio no
adivina la tirada–quizás el poeta.

Tiene razón quien dice: "El resto del poema es el futuro,
que existe fuera de vuestra percepción."

Aunque podría decir "En el destino, no en el dado de oro."
Con eso basta. A cada jugador su turno.»

The Die:

(Joan Brossa)

– "'I imagine you're worried about your fate and worried the
sage can't read the dice' – supposes the poet.

It makes sense, what's been said: 'All that's left of the poem is
the future, which lies outside our perception.'

Although you might say "In destiny, not in a golden die."
Enough then. Each player in turn."

La hormiga:

(Teresa Cerda)

−«Lo pequeño encierra grandes dimensiones. No hay nada que no sea hormiga sin dejar de ser, al mismo tiempo, lo que sea.

Mis manos: yo; la hilera que bulle en el tronco del árbol: yo; y los granos de trigo, y el de arena, y las hojas de parra...

Tenemos perfiles complejos que el ojo no ve ni la cabeza alcanza. Qué importa: ceguera y desazón también somos yo misma.»

The Emmet:

(Teresa Cerda)

– "What's small accommodates large dimensions. Whatever we call an ant doesn't cease to be, at the same time, what is.

My hands: I myself; the teeming line along the trunk of the tree: I myself; and grains of wheat, of sand, fig leaves. . .

We have complex profiles the eye doesn't glimpse nor does the mind comprehend them. What matters: that I'm likewise blindness and apprehension."

La mosca:

−«La insistencia es virtud y condena. 'Insiste en tu ruina
y encontrarás tu salvación' − dejó dicho un poeta.

Se acepta el hambre y el frío, pero la insatisfacción es
cuchillo que se clava uno mismo.

Un mundo pequeño y miserable, el deseo lo transforma en
rica miel: ella nos incita y ella nos sacia, ella también nos
entierra.»

The Fly:

– "What's emphasized is virtue and conviction. 'You insist on your ruin and find your salvation'–as a poet said.

We accept hunger and cold, but dissatisfaction stabs us through the heart.

A miserable little world, desire transforms it into glorious honey: it provokes us and quenches us, and it buries us."

El caballo:

(Augusto Monterroso)

–«Mienten quienes dicen que son libres porque nadie les
maneja. Oigo decir que hubo caballos sin amo, pero pienso
en sus jinetes.

También el que clava tu herradura y te ensilla lleva a
lomos la bota que le espolea.»

The Horse:

(Augusto Monterroso)

– "They lie who claim they're free and no one holds their reins.
I've heard it said there are unmastered horses, but I think about
their riders.

And the rider, who nails your shoes to your hooves and
saddles you, brings to your flanks the boots that spur him on."

El cazo:

(Pedro Núñez)

– «Lo que contienes no basta: un minuto de más y tu propio entusiasmo apagará tu fuego.

'Simple como un anillo' – dirá quien desconoce ; cambia de opinión quien entra en ti: el fondo está en contacto con las llamas»

The Pot:

(Pedro Núñez)

– "What it contains isn't enough: one minute more and your
own enthusiasm will douse the fire.

'Easy as pie' – someone who doesn't know you might say;
but in your shoes, he would change his mind: there are
flames licking the background."

La araña:

—«La red es memoria que todo lo envuelve, y todo lo trae
hacia sí y en sí lo conserva y lo atrapa. Lo que roza su
borde toca el centro mismo.

Repites tu malla y cuando intentas variar tu patrón,
reincides, porque ninguno es mejor que el que te ata.

Sólo el equilibrista puede escapar; el equilibrista, que se
juega la vida cuando pone en peligro las vidas ajenas.»

The Spider:

– "The web is all-encompassing memory and brings everything to itself, holding it in and trapping it. What grazes the edge also touches the center.

You repeat your pattern and when you try to vary the template, you relapse, because none is better than the one that binds you.

Only an acrobat can escape; the acrobat, who risks his life as he endangers the lives of others."

El azúcar:

−«También lo dulce se corrompe y hiede. No hagas nunca promesas de amor.

Un poco de miel ayuda a la medicina; un poco basta para el veneno.

Pero puestos a morir, mejor hacerlo con la miel en los labios.»

The Sugar:

– "What's sweet also rots and stinks. Never make promises of love.

A spoonful of honey helps the medicine. . . ; just a little suffices for poison.

But being put to death, it's best to go with honey on your lips. "

El agua:

—«El deseo es verdad que nadie detiene: sumerge a todo el
que se interpone. Cualquier contra es cauce en su carrera
hacia la mar. Siempre por el camino de menor resistencia.

Las gotas son el origen del río; cantan unidas cuando el
cauce se las lleva.

Al nadador, que monta el agua sin rienda ni brida, ¿de qué
le servirá querer frenar la fuente? Y si lo intenta, ¿qué
podría el agua responder? Nada.»

The Water:

– "Desire it's true can't be held back: it swamps anything
in its way. Anything that stands against it is channeled
into its surge toward the sea. Always on the path of least
resistance.

Droplets are the origin of the river; they sing in harmony
as they are flurried into the main channel.

To the swimmer, who rides the water without reins or bridle,
what's the point of trying to stopper the source? And if
he tries, how could the water respond? Nothing."

Julia Piera

Julia Piera (Madrid, 1970) has published the books *Conversaciones con Mary Shelley* (Icaria, 2006), *Al vértice de la arena* (Biblioteca Nueva, 2003) and *Igual que esos pájaros disecados* (Hojas de Zenobia, 2004). Her most recent poetry collection, *Puerto Rico Digital* (Bartleby, 2009), won the Villa de Madrid 2010 Prize and was a finalist for the Ausiàs March Prize and the National Critics Prize. With a degree in economics from UCM and a Masters in Romance Languages from Harvard, she has published in international magazines including *Poetry Ireland Review, Poeti e Poesía, Revista Galerna* and *Periódico de Poesía* (UNAM). She is the co-screenwriter, with Amalia Iglesias Sema, of the documentary *Antonio Gamoneda, escritura y alquimia*. She also writes for *El Viajero*, the travel section of the newspaper *El País*.

Hay apartamentos vacíos en ese caserío. Algunos habitantes encienden la radio por la noche y bailan con los ausentes. Otros tapian la única terraza de su apartamento para no ver los condominios medioburgueses que los circundan. Y alquilan un telescopio roto para mirar las ventanas de enfrente. En Navidad compran luces de colores y las instalan en la fachada. Hay una cancha de baloncesto cubierta, desteñida, destartalada, rota, donde juegan los diez niños que quedan, día y noche, solos. Una tarde, a la caída del sol, se escuchó un balazo.

Sólo un violento puede asomarse al balcón.

There are empty apartments in the hood. Some residents turn on the radio at night and dance with those who are missing. Others wall up the terrace of their apartment to block out the semi-bourgeois condominiums that surround them. And they rent a broken telescope to get a view through the windows. At Christmas they buy colored lights and hang them in front. There's an indoor basketball court, unpainted, shabby, busted up, where the ten children who stay there night and day play alone. One evening, at sundown, a gunshot went off.

Only the violent step out to the balcony.

Ofrece un resumen a través de su perra:
>"no distingue entre el amor y la cocaína"
>marcha desahuciado huracán o animal urbano
>corrosivo

>¿a qué paloma envenenar si se clonan con el viento?
>¿a qué rata cortar el rabo
>si chillan, fotocopiadas bacterias,
>antes de cocinar, los chinos, sus dientes?

She offers her resume through her bitch:
>"doesn't distinguish between love and cocaine"
>terminal hurricane pace or corrosive urban animal

>what pigeon to poison if they clone it with wind?
>which rat's tail to chop
>if they squeal?, photocopied bacteria,
>before cooking, the Chinese, their teeth?

Y así comienza de nuevo,
            con la política del miedo sobre los hombros
            dientes sudorosos de rabia
            un pecho hecho esgrima de llanto

            entre basuras, *screen*,
            cúmulos súcubos de basuras...
            el terror con un cursor en la manito quemada
            salvapantallas, multietnias
            "personalizadas", por ella,

            ante un balcón blanco
                        de rejas y pitas
                                    salta la b.,
                                                gladiola digital,

                                                y en algo inmenso
                                                se sumerge

And so it begins again,
            lugging the politics of fear on her shoulders
            teeth sweating pure rage
            a chest for the fencing of sobs

            between garbage, *screen,*
            cumulus succubus of garbage . . .
            the terror with a cursor in its burned little hand
            screensavers, multiethnic
            "personalized," just for her,

            from a white balcony
                        of grates and pitas
                                    the b. skips,
                                                digital gladiolus

                                    and something
                                    immense
                                    plunges

Una mañana vuelve pronto, madruga,
    descubre otra gladiola digital, crecida, su raíz al
    ordenador.

    Híbrida. Reprueba con el movimiento de su única hoja,
    burbuja redonda, tripa espejo de la pantalla misma
    abierta como un abanico *imax* hacia ella,

    planear con dedos planisferio
    esta isla patchwork
    su vientre cosido a pasaportes

    los mundos verdes,
    botánicas gigantes en Utuado,
        urgencia de una palabra alimento
            teclea
            "reserva", "guineo", "platanar"

Returning quickly one morning, dawn,
>discovering another digital gladiolus, grown, its root in
>the computer.

>Hybrid. Reproving with each movement of its single
>leaf,
>round bubble, inner mirror of the display itself
>opening toward her like an *imax* fan,

>making plans with planispheric fingers
>this patchwork island
>its guts stitched to passports

>the green worlds,
>botanical giants in Utuado,
>>an urge for a food word
>>typing
>>"preserve," "Guinean," "banana plantation"

While she fell out of Arizona

sin rito o protocolo
un mausoleo de ánforas catalogadas

"mesoamérica", lo llaman.

Enséñame, b., la infamia
sostenida en un puñado de hielo.

While she fell out of Arizona

with neither ritual nor protocol
a mausoleum of catalogued amphoras

"mesoamerica," they call it.

Teach me, b., the infamy
contained in a handful of ice.

Olía la vida container
en sus frascos de crema
ofrendas de aquel cuerpo desparramado
mordía tras la oreja
mientras pensaba
"yo creo que carecía de lenguaje"

luego se daba la vuelta, calor, giraba sus tres caderas,
párpados rendidos al carrusel de la habitación,
"aquí dormiré bien"

whiff of life contained
in her bottles of cream
offerings for that squandered body
it was nibbling at her ear
while she thought
"perhaps it needs some language"

then she turned, all heat, swinging her three hips,
her eyelids captivated by the carousel of the room,
"I'll sleep well here"

"este es un estado desgraciado",
cuando nos persiguen las ratas buscamos el origen
de un origen inexistente de origen

pierde su pasaporte
azul, maduro, cae
al fondo de una isla
con el ruido de su cuerpo página
ombligo pinchado henchido
de insertar tinta y arena
a chascas de sol
en su agujero-carne

loca.

"huele a hierro,
 loca,
  el cuerpo página"

Isla en corte leucocito
        caer y rodar

        " loca, tú sí..."

        coágulo de documento

                por la pendiente

"this is an awful condition"
while rats trail us we're looking for the source
of a source that has no source

she loses her passport
blue, ripe, she falls
to the bottom of an island
with the noise of her page body
belly button pierced swollen
from inserting ink and sand
mixed with sun
into her meat-hole

screwball.

"Smells like iron,
 screwball,
 the page body."

Island in a leukocyte corner
            falling and rolling

            "Screwball, yeah you ..."

        document's coagulum

                    hanging in there

También JRJ trató del comercio de nubes. Allí encontramos piezas de poema en prosa, en la isla de la simpatía, sentadas en el banco de la plaza de Río Piedras, con el cuello doblado hacia atrás y la vista puesta en el trasiego celeste.

Cegaba la dimensión de esas transacciones blancas, el imparable negocio del cielo con unas nubes tan densas. ¿Nos viste, JRJ, alguna vez en la isla?

Había un niño con muletas y el pie gangrenado que vendía MM's y un chico comido por la heroína que se acercó a pedirnos pesetas. Le ofreciste la voluntad en forma de metal. Y él te dio a cambio un MANOJO DE ALGODÓN

JRJ also worked the cloud racket. There we'll find pieces of prose poem, on the island of sympathy, seated on a bench in the plaza of Rio Piedras, neck bent back and gaze fixed on the celestial commotion.

Blinded by the size of such white transactions, the sky's stopless business with its dense clouds. Did you notice us, JRJ, even once on that island?

There was a boy with crutches and a gangrenous foot selling M&M's and a boy consumed by heroin who came up asking us for pesetas. You offered him some goodwill in its metallic form. And for change he gave you a
HANDFUL OF COTTON

Antes de que las olas sinteticen la historia
prefiero agradecer el instante trans-expre-
sionista frente a una litografía y dos objetos.

Ahora siguen en el museo de Miramar.
Mujeres tropicales aumentadas en héroes
de cómic, de gigante negritud, caderas nara-
njas anchas como para taladrar el suelo,
tela en relieve, dos fragmentos segregados
y unidos por el abrazo eléctrico de pelo
azul. ¿Encima de qué sexo, esa "S", serpi-
ente, ansia, dispersa? Los muslos abiertos
cuelgan en exposición para que los ojos fijen
un "yo" / "I" que no reconozco.

El palimpsesto comienza en esta diminuta
perla en un cofre de cristal. Tú, aislada como
el ceceo en el continente, sin rosa de los
vientos, contenida en un jardín andaluz y
ahora expuesta atlántica, amplías el marco
dúctil más allá de la costa, la ceiba, el flam-
boyán. Y mientras ella fotografía tus manos,
tú vuelves a AQUEL AMOR QUE TODAVÍA PASEA

Before the waves smooth out history, I'd like to enjoy a trans-expressionist moment in front of a lithograph and two objects.

Now they can be found in the Miramar museum. Tropical women augmented as comic heroes, gigantically black, orange hips wide enough to guide a drill into the dirt, background material, two fragments separated and joined by a blue-haired electric hug. On top of which sex, that "S," serpent, unease, slips in. Splayed thighs displayed so that the eyes discern an "I" / "I" don't recognize.

The palimpsest begins with this tiny pearl in a glass box. You, isolated as the continental lisp, without your compass rose, boxed off in an Andalusian garden and now exposed to the Atlantic, you extend the ductile mark farther down the coast, the ceiba tree, the poinciana. And while she photographs your hands, you turn back to THE LOVE THAT KEEPS ON GOING

Viajaron a Bruselas para celebrar el ingreso. Mil novecientos ochenta y seis. Iban siete autobuses y todos querían hablar muy alto en los últimos asientos. En Irún entraron perros policía, husmearon. Ana se sentó en un escaño azul del Parlamento, encendía y apagaba el micrófono con el dedo índice como una cremallera instantánea que descosiera el silencio. Cerca de la Grande Place cambiaban pesetas con una calculadora solar.

Mil novecientos noventa y seis. Encerrados en colmenas simétricas preparamos informes sobre países ACP. La moqueta de agricultura era marrón y la de pesca azul. En la foto de grupo europeo todos comíamos, asépticos, lo mismo de la misma loza blanca. Jessica enseñaba sueco en el Matongé para convertirnos en idiomas integrados y figuras superrealistas de cine mudo. También ellas estaban en esa pantalla onírica, fantasmagórica, de ángel a demonio y viceversa, con un mapa de Mercator sin catalogar entre los dedos,

EXCESO DE EXPROPIACIÓN

They traveled to Brussels to celebrate getting in. Nineteen eighty-six. There were seven buses and everyone wanted to talk really loudly in the back seats. In Irún, police dogs boarded, sniffing. Ana sat down on a blue seat near Parliament, flicking the microphone on and off with her index finger as though she were sliding a zipper from a seam of silence. Near La Grande Place they exchanged pesetas for a solar calculator.

Nineteen ninety-six. Shut away in modular hives we prepared reports on the ACP countries. The wall-to-wall carpeting for agriculture was green and the one for fishing was blue. In the European group photo, we were all eating, aseptic, pale as the pale china. Jessica taught Swedish in Matongé trying to persuade us to appreciate integrated idioms and super-realistic characters in silent films. They too drifted across that oneiric, phantasmagoric screen, from angel to devil and vice versa, with an uncatalogued map of Mercator between their fingers,
EXCESS EXPROPRIATION

Ana Gorría

Born in Barcelona in 1979, she has published the poetry collections *Clepsidra* (2004), *Araña* (El gaviero, 2005), and *De lo real y su contrario* (2007), *El presente desnude* (Santiago de Chile: Cuadro de tiza ediciones, 2011) and *La soledad de las formas* (Sol y sombra, 2013). Her work has been included in various anthologies in Spain, Chile, and Peru and has been translated into German, French, English, and Italian. With Raúl Díaz Rosales, she edited a collection of stories and poems called *Cartoemas* (2010) and the *Alpha* and *Omega* volumes for the Catalogue Valverde 32. She serves as an advisory editor for the Mexican journal *Metropolis* and for the web-based literary journal *Los noveles*. With James Womack, she edited and translated a selection of poems, *Travesia esceptica*, by the British poet John Ash, and different versions of the Galician poet Chus Pato as *Hordas de escritura, seguido de Secesión*. She is completing her Ph.D. in Literary Studies at UCM in Madrid. At present, she is on a fellowship from the Foundation for Science and Innovation, but she normally works as a researcher in training at CSIC.

Ovillo

Como una cucaracha boca arriba, roza la voz las cosas,
tocándolas en vano.

Como madeja sucia de hilo negro, la voluntad baldía.
Soñar y deshacerse.

Y lejos, el fantasma que condena. El látigo apagado.
Los naufragios.

Ball

A cockroach on its back, my voice grazes things
without getting any purchase on them.

A filthy tangle of black thread, unplugged desire.
To dream and to come apart.

And beyond, the ghost with its sentence. The whip drawn back.
The wrecks.

Escombrada

Es la cornisa rota y el mundo que se cae.

Igual que el sueño, vuelve
la tarde a ser carne apagada,
cáncer en las paredes de la luz.

Oscuridad que tiembla en un alambre.

Rubble

It's the broken cornice and the world that collapses.

As in a dream, the afternoon
goes back to being mute flesh,
a cancer in the walls of light.

Darkness trembling on a wire.

Fallo

Rimski-Korsakov

Habitación nocturna y voz descalza, con la voz amarilla,
dislocada,
en la niebla, vuelve temprano a casa con los pasos baldíos
y quebrados
a organizar su espacio entre dos tierras rotas, como el invierno,
tan desnuda,
tan frágil,
tan desnuda,
que la librará el frío de su juicio septentrional y exhausto
y excesivo,
para acogerse al duelo del agosto encendido y las quimeras.

Failure

Rimsky-Korsakov

Night room and the discalced voice, with the yellow voice,
dislocated,
in the fog, returning home early, steps bare and
broken
to rearrange the space between two ruined lands, a kind of
    winter,
so naked,
so fragile
so naked,
that the cold is absolved of its boreal and exhausted and
    excessive
verdict,
and takes shelter in August's mourning and mirages.

[Les Noces Barbares]

Marion Hansel

Habitación naranja. Las dos sombras
se arrastran y se muerden. Con la sangre
se enfrentan con la sangre. Todo
es azul, verde, narranja, verde. Todo
y el nocturno terror de conocerse.

[Les Noces Barbaros]

Marion Hansel

Orange room. The two shadows
turn on themselves biting. In blood
they confront the blood. Everything
goes blue, green, orange, green. Everything
and the nocturnal terror of knowing it.

Fuerza de la Erosión

Respiración:
                    la lenta

incertidumbre

de las cosas.

La desnudez del aire, su recelo
de arena movediza.

Casi

de piel mojada.

Negro metal que teme
su roce con la tierra.

Erosion Force

Respiration:

                    the slow

uncertainty

of things.

Nakedness of air, its quicksand
misgiving.

Almost

wet skin.

A black metal that dreads
its brush with the earth.

Et Caetera

En la orilla del ojo pasan coches.

Semáforos.
Obstáculos.

Tal vez la voz cansada,
su descomposición.

El corazón de los cansados sabe.

Etcetera

At the corner of the eye, passing cars.

Stoplights.
Barriers.

Maybe a worn out voice,
its decomposition.

At their cores, the exhausted comprehend.

Umbilical

a José, bien venido

Estación transparente resuelta en luz y herida,

Lento espacio sin voz
abriéndose a la tierra.

Canción hasta el dolor, sueño de cal:
ardiendo

qué hilo no nos separa de la nada.

Umbilical

for José, welcome

The transparent season brings light and torment,

Slow voiceless space
opening into the earth.

Song of regret, torrid dreams:
praying

that the thread doesn't keep us from nothingness.

Más Escarcha en la Noche

Para Jordi

Días en que la vasta desaparición
vuelve como la noche al mediodía.

Temblor

de lo no sucedido.

Algo desliza su jardín en ciernes:
lengua adentro, la piel y el corazón,

el ángulo, la sombra.

Formas de hacerse en la melancolía.

More Frost in the Night

for Jordi

Days in which a vast extinction
comes on like night to the afternoon.

A temblor

from which nothing follows.

Something slinks from the blossoming garden:
core language, skin and heart,

the angle, the shadow.

Forms sliced out of desolation.

Sola en el Centro del Lenguaje

Sin nada que sostenga las manos las palabras su vacío

corre la luz igual que
cae el cansancio igual que
rueda el día igual que

aquí

el temblor de lo esperable

pero ciega
la lengua arde en silencio: voz en nada

Apart in the Pit of Language

Without anything sustaining the hands the words their vacancy

light runs even as
boredom runs even as
day rolls around even as

here

the temblor of the unhoped for

though blind
the tongue smolders in silence: nothing's voice

Capricho Y Semejanza

Igual que cae la voz sobre
las cosas,
así el hacha en la herida
transparente
acaricia el amor, para qué
se desbrozan los caminos las piedras el corazón sol
edad
que despliega las aftas como rosas salvajes
en la sien o en el llanto
la distancia ha aprendido a quemar
la lengua en los oídos,
las preguntas se cierran contra un muro
alrededor del que
la música golpea con la impaciencia hostil
de los objetos
como el hacha la voz

Caprice and Likeness

Just as the voice falls
over things,
the hatchet in the transparent
gash
is a stroke of love, so that
rocks clear the roads the heart sol-
itude
its ulcers arranged like wild roses
at the temple or in tears
distance has learned to burn
language into the ears,
questions fold against a wall
around which
music thrums with the jittery pique
of things themselves
such as the hatchet the voice

Golpes 1

Nombre tras nombre han ido las murallas dejándose caer.
Abiertas las heridas, rotos los corazones transparentes, sí sol, sí
voz, sí aire, rotos los corazones transparentes, arrojados al hielo,
atrapados al vuelo, mariposas de bronce sorprendidas. Sí hubo
un lugar de llanto tan fácil a las nubes, tan parecido al alba y a
la noche, como una casa ardiente que amanece después en la
colina, allí encontró fatiga la canción, descanso el vértigo, Como
desvanecidas las murallas, sólo la soledad de los ojos abiertos
ante palabras blancas, contra palabras blancas, ha herido de
impaciencia este cansancio lento, esta aspereza hundida por
el sol, donde un pájaro roto adelanta su vuelo en los espinos
incapaz de salvarse. Aunque el abismo es ciego y no conoce.
Aunque el abismo es ciego.

Blows 1

Name after name has vanished leaving the walls to crumble.
Open sores, the transparent ruptured core, yes sun, yes voice,
yes air, the transparent ruptured core, disgorged onto ice,
caught on the wing, snagged bronze moths. Yes there was a
grief place as natural as the clouds, near to dawn and night, like
a burning house that appears afterwards on the hill, there where
the song wore out, where vertigo took a break, defeated like
walls, only the solitude of open eyes before white words, against
white words, and this dreary fatigue dying of impatience, this
coarseness sunk deep by the sun, where a broken bird aims
itself at the thorns on which it will die. Although the abyss is
blind and unknown. Although the abyss is blind.

Pilar Fraile Amador

Pilar Fraile Amador (Salamanca 1975) has a Ph.D. in Philosophy from University of Oviedo and a Masters from University of Salamanca. A Professor of philosophy at Enseñanza Secundaria, she also works as an editor. In 2005, she was awarded the Poetry Prize from the University of Zaragoza. Her publications include *El límite de la ceniza* (Prensas universitarias de Zaragoza), *Larva* (Editorial Amphibia), *La pecera subterránea* (Ediciones Amargord) and *Larva seguido de Cerca* (Amargord, 2012). Her work has also been collected in the homage for José Ángel Valente, *Pájaros raíces* (Abada Editores), and in the anthology *La república de la imaginación* (Legados Ediciones). For three years, she directed events for the Association Indómita (http://redindomita.blogspot.com) and she co-directed a poetry program on radio in Madrid.

Primera parte

I

por la tarde bajamos a jugar al vertedero. entre el moho y el
ácido clorhídrico. patas de insecto. siempre a punto de cortarnos
con tapaderas oxidadas. a punto de contraer enfermedades. de
tener las rodillas adornadas de pus. las ratas llegan en manada.
se zambullen en los neumáticos casi convertidos en arena.
sobre los restos de petróleo y plástico derretido alimentan a sus
crías. el resto de animales minúsculos anidan a la orilla de ríos
de ácido magenta y amarillo. humeante savia que baja hasta
el borde de la montaña de desechos. de pronto ya no hay luz y
alguien pregunta qué hacemos aquí. el miedo nos sorprende en
medio de la risa.

2

lo trajeron por la noche y lo encerraron en la cuadra grande. la
que cobija las herramientas en desuso. donde antes iban a beber
los animales. nos llamaron al despertar para que fuéramos a ver
el prodigio. entramos tambaleándonos.
como borrachos. por la emoción.
intentamos acostumbrarnos a la luz arenosa y al rumor de las
termitas que desde hacía años devoraban las vigas. y esperamos.
escuchando ese sonido desconocido. esa respiración baja y
asfixiante.

quisieron proceder al sacrificio.

ese ser oculto entre los restos de paja y excrementos. condenado
a vivir en la habitación de las termitas. ese ser que se lamentaba.
no podía quedarse con nosotros.

First Part

1

in the afternoon we go down to play at the landfill. between the
mold and hydrochloric acid. insect legs. always close to cutting
ourselves on rusty lids. on the verge of illness. finding our
knees adorned with pus. the rats come out in packs. they plunge
through tires decomposing in sand.
on the detritus of melted plastic and oil they nurse their litters.
other tiny animals nest at the edge of magenta and yellow acid
rivers. a steaming sap that dribbles down the mountain of tail-
ings. then there's no light and someone asks what we're doing
here. a tine of fear pierces the fat of our laughter.

2

they brought him in at night and locked him in the big room.
where they keep old tools. where animals used to go for water.
they shouted for us to wake up because we were going to see
the prodigy. we lurched forward.
as though we were drunk. with emotion.
we tried to get used to the grainy light and the sound of termites
that have been chewing the beams for years. and we waited.
hearing that weird sound. that shallow breathing and choking.

they wanted to get on with the sacrifice.

that living being who is hidden in dregs of straw and dung.
condemned to occupy a room quivering with termites.
that being full of pity for himself. who couldn't stick it out with
us.

Segunda parte

I

los cazadores aparecen en los días más fríos del invierno.
huellas de barro en la entrada de la casa. cuerpos de pieles
grisáceas que cuelgan de los ganchos oxidados de la pared de
la cocina. cercos rojizos en la mesa de madera que gotean por
las rendijas y alcanzan el suelo. dibujos de estrellas. dibujos
de monstruos marinos que hemos visto en sueños. esa misma
noche.
las mujeres se mueven deprisa y en silencio. los cazadores se
han sentado junto al fuego y miran con unos ojos que no hemos
visto nunca. hay algo rojo también en sus miradas. algo que
gotea y duele.
las mujeres arrancan las pieles. cuelgan de nuevo los animales
en los ganchos y se encierran allí con todos los ojos negros
desprovistos de luz. en el suelo las sombras de los pequeños
cuerpos. los cazadores empiezan a levantarse a emitir sonidos
guturales a tocarse con deleite algunas zonas del cuerpo.
entonces corremos a escondernos en la cocina entre sus paredes
resbaladizas y agrias. cubiertas de grasa y moho donde las
mujeres vuelven a hacer de la muerte algo comestible.

Second part

I

the hunters show up on winter's coldest days. muddy footprints
in the entranceway. grey-furred bodies dangling from rusty
hooks in the wall of the kitchen. on the wooden table reddish
rings seep through cracks and drip to the floor. pictures of stars.
pictures of sea monsters we've seen in dreams. that very night.
the women move quickly, softly. the hunters are seated by the
fire, staring with eyes like we've never seen before. there's some-
thing red, too, in their eyes. something that drips and aches.
the women tear away the skins. re-hanging the animals on
hooks, they are encircled by snuffed black eyes. across the floor,
the shadows of small bodies. the hunters start to get up making
guttural sounds as they touch, in delight, certain parts of their
bodies. which is when we run to hide ourselves in the kitchen
between the slick, austere walls. covered in grease and mildew
as the women return to make from death something edible.

2

acabamos acurrucándonos en el suelo esperando a que los
hombres vuelvan.

hemos corrido como insomnes excitados por el olor del humo
de los rastrojos. subiéndonos a los tejados. para ver. las mujeres
y los ancianos se han abrazado a nosotros. mirando como
cachorros enfermos. sudando. hemos querido apartarlos. ir
hacia la montaña fosforescente. meter las manos en su luz.
pero hay una cerca invisible. algo que nos impide alejarnos
de las casas. empezamos a sudar. es sofocante el calor de los
últimos días de verano y el aire ennegrecido empieza a afec-
tarnos. a encoger nuestros pulmones que de repente duelen.
algo que no había ocurrido antes.

las mujeres y los ancianos han metido a los animales en las
cuadras y ellos gimen y dan golpes contra el suelo. y parece que
no vaya a para nunca. parece que vayan a seguir golpeando las
puertas llenando todo de polvo y olor a orín.

parece que vayamos a estar siempre aquí intentando contemplar
entre el humo la ladera en llamas.

2

we've just huddled on the floor to wait for the men to come
back.

we've bolted like insomniacs aroused by the smell of smoke
from the stubble. carrying us up to the rooftop. so we might
see. the women and the old ones have hugged us. watching like
sick puppies. sweating. we've wanted to separate them. to make
our way toward the phosphorescent mountain. to reach into
the light. but there's an invisible fence. something that keeps us
from leaving the houses. we start to sweat. it's suffocating, the
swelter of late summer, and the blackened air starts to get to us.
to shrivel our lungs which suddenly ache. which is something
that's never happened before.

the women and the old ones have been leading the animals to
their stalls where they wail and stamp. and it seems they won't
stop. it seems they're likely to kick through the doors, filling
everything with dust and the reek of urine.

it seems that we'll always be here struggling, through the
smoke, to make out the hillside on fire.

Parte 1: Cerca

hasta las crías más torpes saben apartar de sí a los parásitos.
al caer la tarde la fiebre asciende por las piernas hasta llegar
al pecho. las mujeres corren. traen trapos rojos empapados en
agua. susurran. se miran. apoyan las manos en nuestro pecho.
en los ojos. en el vientre. se hunden a los pies de la cama.
afuera vuelan los vencejos. quieren entrar en nosotros. anidar
en nosotros. vuelan desde nuestro pecho y salen al cielo como
serpientes con alas.
una sombra espera detrás de la puerta. agria como los limones
que comemos sumergidos en miel.
somos un bulto que gruñe debajo de las sábanas. empapadas
violáceas. nuestro dolor no limpia.

Part 1: Hedge

even the runt of the litter knows how to pluck its own parasites.
as evening falls the fever rises from our thighs to our chest. the
women run off. they return with sopping red rags. they whisper.
looking on. holding their hands to our chest. to our eyes. to
our belly. they collapse at the foot of the bed. outside the swifts
careen. yearning to enter us. to nest in us. they burst from our
breast back out into the sky like winged snakes.
a shadow lingers behind the door. sour as those lemons we drip
with honey to eat.
we are a lump growling under the sheets. soaked purple. the
source of our pain unclear.

hay un rincón en la casa bañado por la luz. allí vamos a secarnos el cabello. en el suelo se va formando una mancha como de hilos amontonados sobre la tierra húmeda. el peine de púas finísimas una y otra vez recorre el cuero cabelludo para asegurarse de que todo está limpio.

nadie sabe cuánto tiempo pasamos así. sin mirarnos. al salir reímos como crías de pájaro. (nos damos palmadas en la espalda).

there's a corner of the house swathed in light. which is where
we go to dry our hair. on the floor there's a stain expanding like
a mound of wires in wet dirt. the fine-toothed comb again and
again rakes the scalp so that everything goes clean.
no one knows how much time we spend this way. not looking
at ourselves. going out we shriek like baby birds with laughter.
(patting ourselves on the back).

en ocasiones nos acercamos a la ciénaga. despacio.
con cuidado de no rozar las ortigas. contenemos la respiración
para que el veneno no penetre en la sangre y las avispas no
huelan el sudor.
el terreno se reblandece a medida que nos acercamos y hay que
quitarse los zapatos y sostenerlos en la mano.
una vez en el lodo caminamos más seguros. como animales
anfibios. con branquias. fluctuante sonido del barro a medida
que nos adentramos en las partes más oscuras y frías de la
ciénaga. risas nerviosas. chirridos de pájaros atrapados en los
arbustos anegados por la última crecida.
y de pronto la sensación de que algo. de que alguien. se ha
hundido en el barro.

sometimes we head to the swamp. slowly.
careful not to brush the nettles. holding our breath so the
poison won't seep into our blood and the wasps won't scent our
sweat.
the ground goes soft the closer we get until we have to pull off
our shoes and hold them in our hands.
when we hit the mud, we can walk better. like amphibious
animals. gilled. oscillating sounds of mud as we make our
way into the darkest and coldest parts of the swamp. nervous
laughter. chirps of birds trapped in bushes waterlogged in the
last flood.
and suddenly the sense that something. that someone. has been
sucked under.

Parte ii: Solar

en el solar de arena y excrementos con sus botas ceñidas sobre
el pantalón de lana el hombre alimenta a las crías.
lo espiamos agachados entre las zarzas. los animales inmensos
se acercan a la piedra magenta y lamen en la parte hundida.
todos se mueven despacio como si tuvieran piedras en el estó-
mago. la leche sale por los chupadores metálicos. los animales
lamen mientras la leche va por el conducto a un lugar descono-
cido. las crías comen de la mano del hombre hasta que agotan
los granos dorados. él se pasa esa misma mano por la frente
como si estuviera cansado o de pronto hubiese recordado algo.
respiramos sin notar en los pies el aguijón de las espigas.

Part II: A Lot

on the lot full of sand and excrement with his boots tucked into
wool trousers the man is feeding the brood.
we spot him squatting in the bushes. huge animals draw near
the magenta stone and lick at its hollows. they move as slowly
as if they had stones in their stomachs. milk drips from metallic
feeders. animals licking as the milk runs through the pipe to
who knows where. the chicks pecking at the man's hand until
all the golden kernels are gone. he puts that same hand to his
forehead as though he were tired or suddenly he remembered
something. we go on breathing and don't notice the nettles
stinging our feet.

la partera llega a primera hora. la luz metálica de noviembre entra a través de los visillos. amoratadas las manos los labios a punto de cortarse. corremos sin dirección por el solar acercándonos al lodo y a los abrevaderos. en la charca los zapateros ya no proyectan su sombra de hombres diminutos. ha venido la lluvia con su orden.

damos palmadas bajo el techo de cañizo juntando mucho las manos como si fuéramos a perderlas o a salir volando.

the midwife arrives early. November's metallic light comes in
through the curtains. our hands gone purple our lips ready to
drop off. we run aimlessly through the lot and verge into the
mud and water holes. on the pond the horseflies no longer cast
their little-man shadows. the rain shows up with its order.
we pat the underside of the reed roof all our hands joined as
though we were going to lose them or as though we might take
off flying.

Esther Ramón

Esther Ramón (1970, Madrid) is a poet and critic who earned her
Ph.D. in comparative literature at the Autonomous University
of Madrid. Her work has been widely anthologized and also
published in the discrete volumes: *Tundra* (Igitur, 2002), *Reses*
(Trea, Critical Eye Award 2008), *grisú* (Trea, 2009) and *Sales*
(Amargord, 2011). She is the coordinating editor of the magazine
Minerva and she co-directs a Radio Circle poetry program called
Definición de savia.

subterra

el humo de
las chimeneas
dibuja un óvalo
sobre la roca
el pico los pájaros
en celdas el miedo
al gas dinamitamos
precarias galerías
nos abrimos paso
al ritmo de la
polea el ascensor
de los que descienden
maneja la precisión de
las herramientas
un obstáculo
tangentes
ahora
la sirena

underearth

smoke from
chimneys
inscribes an oval
over the rock
the beak the canaries
in cages fear of
firedamp we dynamite
exquisite galleries
we dig our way
to the rhythm of an
elevator hoist
for those who go down
the mechanisms
are trued by
their obstacle
on a tangent
now
the siren

piedras preciosas

manos de la
extracción sobre
la mesa envueltos
en trapos ordenados
por formas por
tamaños en el suelo
breves pedazos
desechados
rodeamos
los volquetes
apagando
las
linternas
y en silencio buscamos
sus aristas rozándonos
los dedos cerrando
al salir la puerta
con infinito
cuidado

precious stones

extracted by
hand on
the table wrapped
in cloth arranged
by shape by
size on the floor
chipped discarded
pieces
surround us
the dump trucks
snuff out
our lamps
and in quiet we feel for
the chafing edges
as we exit the door
our fingers closing up
with infinite
caution

descorche

al pasar por
ciertos túneles
bufidos el vapor
de los ciervos
que buscan
las fuentes
que nos huelen
tablones clavos
abandono
de vetas
silabeantes
al roce de su
enramado
fetidez que se anticipa
al miedo la combustión
el aire que prende fuera
del alcance
de su aliento

uncorking

snorted through
twinned tunnels
the steam
of deer
sniffing out
the source
of our scent
boards nails
the neglect
of syllabical
veins
that brush against
their own branched
stench they sense
our fear combustion
air snagging just beyond
the reach
of their breath

ensayo

sigilo junto al
horno estéril
todos duermen
la trampilla
cubierta de tierra
y una escalera
oblicua abajo
estatuas nuevas
la sed de la linterna
dibuja elipses
en los sacos vacíos
un rastro de trigo
bajo la herrumbre
de las herramientas
una espantada
de ratas
que argumenta

essay

stealthy by the
sterile stove
everyone asleep
the trapdoor
covered with dirt
and a ladder
slanted down
new statues
the flashlight's thirst
tracing ellipses
over empty bags
a dash of wheat
under the iron taste
of tools
a panic
of rats
squabbles

palabras

detrás de los
árboles niñas
que pintan
sus brazos y
duermen sobre
hojas friccionan
las patas son
grillos liberados
el sol
les arruga
las manos
se remangan
para lavarles
la ropa y sus
pinturas relucen
como gemas venenosas
como luces de nitrato

words

behind the
trees girls
who paint
their arms and
sleep on
leaves rub
their feet are
escaped crickets
the sun
wrinkles
their hands
rolling up sleeves
so they can wash
their clothes and their
paintings gleam
like venomous gems
like nitrate lights

pigmentos

con limas furtivas
rebajamos unos
gramos su peso
sobre el plástico
cubierto nievan
copos de índigo
de terracota
en la superficie
espesaremos
sus tonos
con la saliva
de los caballos
de carga
con las lluvias
brotarán grullas
luminosas en
danza sobre
las paredes

pigments

with furtive rasps
we cut the weight
by a few grams
on the covered
plastic indigo
flakes of terracotta
snowing
over the surface
we muddle
the hue
with saliva
from work
horses
with rain
albescent cranes
pop up
dancing along
the walls

edad del hierro

y con la piedra
a veces pollos
atronados
trilobites
de geometría
intacta
helechos rígidos
dientes
ligeros huesos
pleistocenos
tablillas de cera
y arenisca estacas
raros insectos
suspendidos
en ámbar
conchas astas
talladas raíces
raspadores collares
de sílex plumas
puntas de lanza

Iron Age

and with stone
sometimes chickens
shrieking
trilobites
with their geometries
intact
stiff ferns
teeth
lightweight pleistocene
bones
wax and sandstone
tablets
weird insects
suspended
in amber
shell horns
root cuttings
scrapers necklaces
of flint feathers
spearheads

*   *   *

En el vertedero de caballos todo está listo para la representación.

Encendieron las luces de emergencia y nadie sabía si los que corrían querían salir o venían llegando.

(En realidad estaban detenidos).

Ignoraban el humo, pero su estilizado rostro azul sonreía a los presentes.

Se habían reunido allí para estudiar los cuerpos.

Un carpintero había fabricado siete grandes camillas de madera. Iban a cubrirse con enormes sábanas.

Esto es obra de un demente. Alguien le hizo callar. Los de las batas blancas se adelantaron.

Heridas de cortes desiguales. Los ayudantes anotaban cada detalle y los más virtuosos insertaban dibujos entre las letras.

Los dos primeros animales lucían exactas mutilaciones. El demente había concebido gemelos. Luego individuos únicos.

Todos los caballos eran tordos menos uno blanco que parecía intacto. Pero siguieron la costura. Los órganos estaban desco-locados. Era un orden incomprensible en que el corazón y los riñones se apretaban en la garganta.

La luna adelgazaba aquella noche en que algunos hombres se reunieron en un hangar, mientras los demás dormían.

*   *   *

In the horse dump everything's ready for rendering.

They flicked on the emergency lights and no one knew if they were running to get there or to get away.

(Actually, they were arrested.)

They ignored the smoke, but its sleek blue face grinned at the audience.

They were gathered there to study the bodies.

A carpenter had built seven big stretchers. They were going to cover them with huge sheets.

This is the work of a psycho. Someone shut him up. The ones in white coats picked up their pace.

Gashes of different lengths. The assistants noted every detail and the most virtuous inserted drawings between the letters.

The first two animals exhibited identical mutilations. The psycho had birthed twins. Then they came in ones.

All the horses were dapple-grey except the white one which seemed intact. But they followed the seam. The organs were topsy-turvy, incomprehensibly arranged so the heart and kidneys were jammed into the throat.

The moon thinned out that night as some men collected in a hangar while the rest slept.

Después de taparlos decidieron iniciar las diligencias. El sospechoso podía ser un joven pálido, empleado en un matadero. O un maquinista. O el conductor de un circo itinerante.

Para velarlos dispusieron sillas polvorientas. Apagaron las luces y los cristales del techo se abrieron como ojos en blanco.

Sus pensamientos tomaron senderos diferentes pero todos cabalgaban en el mismo bosque, saltaban obstáculos inverosímiles, inventaban nombres para calmar a sus monturas.

After covering them, they decided to get down to business. The suspect could be a pale young man employed in a slaughter-house. Or a mechanic. Or the driver for a traveling circus.

To keep watch, they set out dusty chairs. The cut the lights and crystals on the ceiling flicked on like eyes.

Their thoughts took different paths but everyone rode through the same forest, jumping incredible obstacles, calming their mounts with made-up names.

*   *   *

Son excrementos secos. O son piedras.

Si son excrementos:

Las mujeres los recolectan en cestos. Para avivar los huertos, los jardines. Para que algo crezca.

Si son piedras:

Las plantarán como semillas y engordará lo muerto, se extenderá en grandes planicies grises.

Se arropan con mantas rojas y los rastrean por toda la playa. Quizá el paso de una caravana de bueyes. Y los surcos sean ruedas. Van a salvarles del hambre. Son excrementos.

Cuentan resignadas las vetas. Hace tiempo que se agotaron los peces. Sopa de algas, carne de gaviota, briznas débiles. Piedras azules para el repecho de las ventanas. Las marrones en la chimenea, rugosas como nueces. En la boca las blancas.

Mientras los suben inventan instrucciones. Suavizarlos con agua. Hervirlos. Un emplasto para las tierras. De pronto una grita con voz de pájaro y tira su cesto. Las otras la toman de los hombros, le devuelven el peso lentamente.

Cada mano es el platillo de una balanza. También hay rocas ligeras. A veces el pasto prensado pesa como las piedras.

El olor se esconde. Siempre se esconde. El sabor se condimenta.

Pero son de una rara belleza. La coleccionista las mira largamente, las acaricia en secreto, las calienta. Se queda con algunas. Como esta que se acerca a la cara, ovalada como un

*   *   *

It is dried excrement. Or it is a pile of stones.

If it is excrement:

Women gather it into baskets. To revive the orchards, the gardens. So something might grow.

If they are stones:

They plant them like seeds and the dead are fattened up, the great plains extended.

They wrap them in red blankets and drag them along the beach. Not unlike a convoy of oxen. And the furrows look like wheeltracks. They mean to save themselves from hunger. It is excrement.

The veins are used up. It's been forever since the fish died out. Seaweed soup, gull meat, anemic toasts. Blue stones for the window ledge. Brown ones for the chimney, rough as nuts. In the mouth, the white ones.

As they lift the stones, they invent instructions. They'll soften them with water. Boil them. A poultice for the land. Suddenly a bird-like voice shrieks and a basket tips. The others lift it from her shoulders, but the weight will soon enough return.

Each hand is a scale. Plus, there are lighter rocks. Sometimes the pressed grass weighs as much as rocks.

The odor hides itself. Always stays hidden. Spicing the taste.

But they are of a rare beauty. A collector, she considers them at length, pets them in secret, warms them up. That's how it is with some. Like this one she touches to her face, oval as a

rostro, en el centro la cuenca vacía de un ojo, una boca, un laborioso agujero. Y por color el viento. Y por fruto.

Si hubiera que tumbarse boca arriba a esperar el beso del ángel. O su espada de plata. O una lluvia de piedras.

Para subir se concentra en la simetría de sus pasos y en las sombras de las otras mujeres. En sus sombras diezmadas.

Después del largo viaje, los carros en la inmensa planicie. Sus bueyes depositan huevos minuciosos. Los pisan. Prosigue el camino.

cameo, with an empty eye at its center, a mouth, a laborious hole. And taking its color from wind. And from fruit.

As if all she could do was lie face-up waiting for the kiss of an angel. Or its silver sword. Or a rain of rocks.

To get up, she concentrates on the symmetry of footsteps and on the shadows of the other women. On their decimated shadows.

After the long journey, so many carts on the vast plain. Their oxen deposit minuscule eggs. They are stomped on. The road keeps going.

J.M. Antolín

J.M. Antolin is a poet and painter. Born in Valladolid, Spain, he now resides in the United States. His books of poetry include: *Cuenco/Bowl* and *El Cuerpo del Libro Quemado/Ojo Vivo/Los Animales extinguidos* (a trilogy). A forthcoming book of poetry; *El Alimento No Humano/Non-Human Nourishment* was written during the last ten years in the United States. Other books include *La Coronacion Eterna/Eternal Coronation*, a catalogue retrospective of J.M. Antolín's paintings and sculptures published by the Spanish Government of Castilla and Leon. A book documenting the process of his commissioned mural-sized painting, *La Membrana/The Membrane* will be published by CIDAUT Foundation. Currently, J.M. Antolín is editing and translating an American poetry anthology spanning the last four decades and completing *Poetry and Empire*, a book of essays of critical theory about the relationship between power and poetics.

Poder de New York

Los tiempos se sitúan – la silla nos acoge –
La lluvia apedrea los pájaros –
Qué es la perfecta canción –
Mi diafragma (tienda de lona) hinchado
Recibe otro ser. Además la placa del continente perpetúa
Otras maderas, vigas del mundo. Muchos seres, inconscientes,
Se cuelan en la cárcel, esta inmensa ciudad cansa
Las mareas venideras con sus muelles, – el robusto son
De la sangre no llega a horadar el ancho muro
De la mentira, y la belleza se soterra – pero aun es llamada
Una vez segunda –
                        Como una piedra mineral dentro de la veta
Tan antigua como otras voces, como el cronómetro dentro de la
estatua. Voz desde lejos;

Y así consigue lo que digo en este instante de tráfico, muy bajo,
    casi inaudible

The Force of New York

The times make their adjustments – the chair welcomes us –
Rain stones the birds –
What is the perfect song –
My inflated diaphragm (canvas tent)
Allows a second presence. Likewise the continental plate
    extends
Other woods, beams of world. There are many who, unaware,
Wash up in prison, this immense city wears down
The coming tides with its wharfs, – the robust come
From blood the drill won't reach the wide wall
Of lies, and beauty buries itself – though we call on it
Again –
            Like mineral source at the vein's core
As old as other voices, as the chronometer in the statue. A voice
    from afar;

And that's why what I say in this trafficked moment, very softly,
    almost inaudible, obtains

Parque Van Cortland y Memoria

I
Larva de flecha viviente
La bandada de gansos salvajes descendiendo a la isla,

La sangre de los seres
Es un mar enfrente de los seres,
(Antaño
 Nunca agotado)

Con una reclinación doy a luz a mi padre,
Es el origen ritual de mi rodilla. Voy a ser arañado

Y configurado por la presa en el altar, no por tiempo
De cálculo, de oración que uno posee –
Sólo por el flujo
Que ahora se registra   con pie de voz desconocida – ¿cómo?

¿Es el trabajo de otro ser
Lo que ahora lo que está ahora sucediendo?
En lo alto – la procesión planetaria
Elige las glándulas de un gusano, de un mamífero inadvertido
Para perpetuarse,
Toldo estoico
Que descansa en mí – el cielo
Me alcanza con frío y me detiene;

Silencio de sed
En cielo,   gestando
Embriones paralelos, tribu de testigos.

La visibilidad de los peces en el delta del rio entrando
Es idéntica a la de las aves, que flotan en lo extremo, dichas para
    siempre,

Van Cortland Park and Memory

I
A living arrow's larva
The flock of wild geese descending onto the island,

The blood of human beings
Is a sea those beings face,
(From long ago
Never exhausted)

Leaning back, I give birth to my father,
It's the ritual origin of my knee. I'll be scraped together

And configured by the prey on the altar, not by time
For calculations, for prayers I might make –
Only by the flow
That registers now   with an unknown voiceprint – so?

Is it someone else's labor
Which now, which only now comes to fruition?
At the peak – the planetary procession
Pepetuates itself
From the glands of a worm, some minor mammal,
That stoic awning, the sky,
Slackens over me – it
Touches me with its cold and stops me in my tracks;

Silence of thirst
In heaven,   gestating
Parallel embryos, a tribe of witnesses.

The visibility of fish in the delta of the river
Rhymes with that of birds, floating in the distances, forever
    spoken,

Y el polvo de carretera dejado atrás en el viaje
Brilla al ascender tocado por el sol rojo y es dicho
Nosotros aceleramos en la sombra con nuestra percusión
Y dibujamos sin luz.

And dust our journey leaves behind in the road
Shines as, brushed by red sun, it rises and is spoken
We speed off into the shadows with our percussion
And we sketch figures in the dark.

2. (Sacramento)

Sacramento, juguete huérfano de hueso, pájaro (altura mayor,
Gota   gota de plata abrazante
Esperando el diamante en el día ocre.
      La arcilla reciente – húmeda, es mi órgano, altura mayor)

Venus, imperceptible   sin el espejo húmedo de la hierba
Mente expoliada y seca   el recinto de luz de la luna
No existe sin la presencia   del joven avellano, en ayuno por un
Mes. Sacramento.

2. (Sacramento)

Sacramento, bone orphan plaything, bird (higher,
Drop   blazing silver drop
Waiting for the diamond from the day's ocher.
          Fresh clay–wet, it's my very organ, plenary)

Venus, imperceptible   without the wet mirror of grass
Mind plundered and dry   the macula of moonlight
Doesn't exist outside the presence   of that hazel boy, fasting
For a month. Sacramento.

3. Sacramento (Génesis)

Hinchó las montañas
En días indisolubles, –

Midió el viento el tamaño
De mi osamenta inadvertida
Mientras yo era formado,

Y cuando la brisa desnudó su brazo
Mis bronquios alcanzaron la costa –
Flora arterial abierta,

La saliva inaugural de los ríos
Fríos – no puede ser imaginada,
Flujo de 248
Articulaciones, igual al cuerpo
Humano, que oía erróneamente
Oscuridad y luz desde un principio,
Postura de la planta de té yogi
Soñando la unión

3. Sacramento (Genesis)

It made the mountains swell
Into indissoluble days, –

The wind sized up
My bones inadvertently
While I took shape,

And when the breeze bared its arm
My bronchi reached the coast –
Arterial flora wide-open,

The inaugural saliva of cold
Rivers – can't be imagined,
Flow of 248
Joints, as in the human
Body, which I heard wrongly
Darkness and light from the start
The stance of the yogi tea plant
Dreaming of union

4. *(Traductor)*

Nadie puede traducir y todo el mundo está traduciendo.

Noche lenta traduce su propio cuerpo, (por delante lenta,) el
ganado turbio traduce para
            alcanzar el agua.
La linterna no está. Pozo viudo, y arroyo rubio que atraviesan las
cosechadoras de óxidos
            escondidos.
Nada puede imitar al trigo adolescente que se escora
Bajo rachas irregulares de brisa, o traducir

Mi dolor alcanzado
Como éxito del sol

4. (Translator)

No one can translate and the whole world is translating.

The torpid night translates its own body, (plodding slowly
forward), cloudy cattle translate
       themselves toward the water.
There's no flashlight. A widowed well, and a blonde stream that
crosses combines of unseen
       oxides.
Nothing can mimic the adolescent wheat that bends
Under irregular gusts of wind, or translate

My pain whelmed
As the sun hit

5. *(Noche Villegouge. La Garonne)*

Falenas transparentes negras en lo negro,
Mi respiración sin familia –

Bajo ramas de higuera nocturnas, oscuras contra el cielo, puras,
Y frutos monosílabos, remotos, – están creciendo.
Si se elevaran por una escala superior
Alcanzarían la otra cara de la montaña, más invisible que
    nunca –

Donde las fronteras verbales, lentas.
Y aunque me muevo silenciosamente, no localizo
Al pájaro que emite esa voz perfecta que parece aturdir
La mente en dos épocas - aunque sólo canta hoy, y extenderse

Desde los paños de roca invernales y refugios
Paleolíticos hasta perennes álamos de estío en mi memoria,
Transformados en cruces de abuelos –

Desde la ruina del patio dislocado en la II gran Guerra
Llega hasta los tallos amparados al borde del cimiento del mar
En cuya máquina de presente se sofoca –
Oscuros   desde mi estatura
Los higos   bogando, hacia quién?
Yo, bogando hacia atrás
Mientras ellos crecen y se parten –
Entregándose a otra corriente.

5. (Villegouge Night. The Garonne)

Transparent black moths in the blackness,
My breathing sans family—

At night, under fig branches, dark against the sky, pure,
And remote, their monosyllabic fruits—are plumping up.
If they hoisted themselves a little higher
They would fall on the other side of the mountain, more
    invisible than ever—

Where the slow, the verbal borders.
And though I move quietly, I can't situate
The bird emitting those perfect notes that stun
My mind across two seasons—although it sings only now, the
    song goes on

From winter shelves of rock and paleolithic
Shelters through the perennial summer poplars in my memory,
Evoking my grandparents' crosses—

From the yard debris dislodged during the Second World War
The song carries toward the border grasses of the cemetery by
    the sea
In whose mechanical present it snuffs out—
Dark   about my height
The fig trees   rowing, to whom?
And me, rowing backwards
As they mature and break away—
Surrendered to another current.

Siete Piedras No Alineadas

Esta primavera–es olor que acogeré como la habitación que
    cerró sus ventanas,
Extendió su imaginación
Y se deshidrató–viajando
Tras aquellos que vivieron un día entre sus muros.

Algo o alguien conoció su propia belleza.

Un martillo deformaba las efigies de los emperadores en las
    monedas,
En antiguas y en las futuras;
Un niño aún con cara de feto
Era el único animal civilizado del Imperio.

Quédate, sumérgete en el largo ataúd y regresa
Triunfal con un sentimiento que no sea un epitafio
Iluminado por el terror de las campanas–
Y había imágenes, había imágenes que parecían de bronce
Cuando la luz retrocedía y renovaban su vibración como parte
    del cielo.

Esta primavera,–con todas sus semanas encima,
Tantos días no visibles
Como un río sobre nuestras cabezas.
                      No tengo un oído
Tan fino como el Inimaginable Todo de la Orquídea–
Un plasma sin necesidad de sus propias palabras;
Aquello que está en el mundo–hacia ella se precipita
O será un mero bulto de su ceguera sin nostalgia.

En la muerte de la Piedra Eterna (base del Templo)
La cabeza humana no oirá
Nada, la cabeza humana soñará con el agua reflejante y vaciada

Seven Stones Not Aligned

This spring – a scent I'll keep close as a room with closed
    windows,
The imagination gone outwards
And gone dry – trailing
Behind those who lived between the walls of a single day.

Someone or something caught on its own loveliness.

A hammer flattened the effigies of emperors on coins,
In ancient times and in futures;
A boy still wet behind the ears
Was the empire's single civilized beast.

Stay a while, lie back in the long coffin and come back
Triumphant with feeling which matters more than any epitaph
Illumined by the terror of bells –
And there were images that took on a bronze glow
When the light faded and its vibrations merged with sky.

This spring, – with all its weeks piled up,
So many invisible days passing
Like a river over our heads.

                I have no ear
As finely tuned as the Unimaginable All of the Orchid –
A plasma with no need for explanation;
What we find in the world, that's what pours itself out
Or is nothing but a bundled blindness, clear of nostalgia.

When the Eternal Stone (the Temple's base) is destroyed
The human head won't hear
Anything, the human head will engender dreams like water,
    reflective and empty

De los paisajes de lo alto –

Nadie esclavizó a nadie en su ojo de amor puro –
La ambición de ese instante es autoinmolación
Que pertenece al fuego de los amantes – en un fuego

Que muere sólo cuando no queda nada de nosotros.

Of the landscapes higher up –

No one enslaved anyone in love's clear eye –
The aim of this moment is self-immolation
Which means the lover's fire – a fire

That dies only when nothing of us remains.

Seis Momentos

Apareándose a lo largo de las costas
Existe la tribu de los cormoranes negros –
Octubre regándolos.

Existe el tiempo de los olmos talados
Como un remo que se siente circundado por el mar;
Los acontecimientos tienen conexiones invisibles.

Existe el sueño con un imposible pan
Caliente – un hijo del cielo
Que venza
Colaborando junto a las ramas podridas de la tierra –
Que lo elevarán, volando con él –
Las astillas disueltas cosiendo una ropa
Para un cuerpo sin muerte.

Mis paralelas cuerdas vocales
Como dos rígidas piedras
En un intervalo que enmarca la niebla –
Un ser cae dentro de su trama – y otro ser está fuera para
    siempre.

Como un aliento inconsciente es la voz susurrante –
Oh, la respiración es una forma.
Sin un nombre, estamos desligados –
Dispersos por la faz de la tierra.
La ciudad quedó sin límites –
Ido el sol, reina la oscuridad. Y he aquí
Que un horno humeante y una antorcha
Encendida pasa entre los cuerpos partidos

Six Moments

Pairing up along the coast,
There's a tribe of black cormorants –
Showered with October.

There's a time of felled elms
Like a paddle that feels surrounded by sea;
Events are invisibly connected.

There's the dream with its impossibly warm
Bread – a child of god
Who gives out
In the dirt with the earth's rotten branches –
Which hold him up, floating him along –
The soggy pulp forming a casing
For his deathless body.

My vocal chords parallel
As two set rocks
In an interval invaded by fog –
Someone falls into the frame – and another winks out forever.

Unconscious as breath, this whispering voice –
Yes, respiration is a form.
Nameless, we come loose –
Scattering across the face of the earth.
The city stretches out without limits –
Gone the sun, the darkness reigning. And it's exactly
Here that a smoking furnace and a snuffed
Torch are passed between severed bodies

Soy la manzana

Soy la manzana de mis bronquios
Cuando ellos se levantan a luchar, –
La resina verdadera de mi garganta, abandonada
Gotea
Para ser cantada y brillada por
Otra región, distante
Y adherencia – completándose

Con mi allí lejano, –
Miel   oscura   seduciendo, Espacio

De la noche, seducido
Por un torso no de mamífero no de un dios
No de árbol – todo, rozado.

Qué lector (estoy) anticipando

Y qué humedad permite a los hocicos
Trabajar
En el nuevo reino.

La voz de al quien que resucita –
es el ladrillo incandescente de un horno
inengendrado;

Una vértebra
Sin carne, acomodándose de nuevo al cielo, volviendo.

La mente   añorando algo que no perdió nunca
gotea también

I'm the Apple

I'm the apple of my lungs
When they get up to fight,—
The real resin of my throat, relinquished,
Drains off
To be sung and polished in some-
Where else, distant
And adhesive—coming full circle

With me there far off—
Dark   seductive   honey,   Space

Of the night, seduced
By a torso neither mammalian nor godly
Nor arboreal—everything touched by it.

What reader (am I) anticipating

And what snouts come to snuffle
Such dampness
In this new kingdom.

The voice of the resuscitated—
Is the incandescent brick in the unbegotten
Oven:

A fleshless
Vertebra, fusing with sky, returning.

The mind   longing for something that won't be lost
Which is draining too

Publication of this work is made possible, in part [hopefully], by the generous support of the Government of Spain, Ministerio de Cultura de España, Subdirrección General de Promoción del Libro.

Antonio Gamoneda's poems "Inebriated, he was...," "He observed the calm...," "An animal hidden...," "New York Divan," "Being in You," "Fragments from Impure Pavane," and "Saturday" were published in *LyrikLine.org.* "Rage" was published in *Spain's Great Untranslated*, edited by Javier Aparicio, Auerlio Major & Mercedes Monmany.

Olvido García Valdés' poems in translation were published in The Miami Rail, Hunter Braithwaite, editor, in Spring 2013.

Miguel Casado's "In the City" was published in *The Wolf* (UK), James Byrne, editor, in Summer 2013.

Marcos Canteli's poems from "Catalogue of the Incessant" appeared in *Mantis*, edited by Bronwen Tate and Joshua Edwards, Spring 2011 and in *Comma*, edited by Pablo Lopez and Amanda LaBerge, 2013.

Sandra Santana's "Actually, Erotic Fantasy...," "Natural History...," and "The Horoscope Eventfully Announces..." appeared in *Fence*, Spring 2012. "Matters about which Unfortunately I Have No Brilliant Opinion to Offer" at *Poem Flow* in 2013.

Benito del Pliego's poems "The Die" and "The Chameleon" appeared in Two Lines, Summer 2012; "The Horse," "The Spider," and "The Fly," appeared in *Two Lines* online edition.

Five untitled poems by Julia Piera ("She offers her resume," "And so it begins again," "Returning quickly one morning," "She smelled the life container" "this is an awful condition") appeared in *Nth Position* (France) in July 2011.

Ana Gorría's poems "Ball," "Apart in the Pit of Language," "[Les Noces Barbaros]," and "Caprice & Likeness" appeared in Circumference, edited by Elizabeth Clark Wessel in 2012. Her poems "Rubble" and "Failure" appeared in The Wolf, edited by James Byrne, in summer 2013.

Pilar Fraile Amador's poems, part 1 and 2 of "Hedge," appeared in *Gulf Coast*, edited by Samuel Amadon, Spring 2012. [Sections 1 and 2 of "A Lot" sent to Narrative Northeast, Pamela Hughes, ed 08-25-13]

Esther Ramon's poems "Unearth," "Words," and "Essay" appeared in *Aldus: a Journal of Translation* in 2012. Circumference published "In the horse dump..." and "It is dried excrement..." in 2012.

J. M. Antolín's poems in translation appeared in *Aldus: a Journal of Translation* in 2011.

Other Titles from Otis Books | Seismicity Editions

Erik Anderson, *The Poetics of Trespass*
    Published 2010 | 112 Pages | $12.95
    ISBN-13: 978-0-979-6177-7-5
    ISBN-10: 0-979-6166-7-4

J. Reuben Appelman, *Make Loneliness*
    Published 2008 | 84 pages | $12.95
    ISBN-13: 978-0-9796177-0-6
    ISBN-10: 0-9796177-0-7

Bruce Bégout, *Common Place. The American Motel*
    Published 2010 | 143 Pages | $12.95
    ISBN-13: 978-0-979-6177-8-2
    ISBN-10: 0-979-6177-8-

Guy Bennett, *Self-Evident Poems*
    Published 2011 | 96 pages | $12.95
    ISBN-13: 978-0-9845289-0-5
    ISBN-10: 0-9845289-0-3

Guy Bennett and Béatrice Mousli, Editors, *Seeing Los Angeles:
A Different Look at a Different City*
    Published 2007 | 202 pages | $12.95
    ISBN-13: 978-0-9755924-9-6
    ISBN-10: 0-9755924-9-1

Robert Crosson, *Signs/ & Signals: The Daybooks of Robert Crosson*
    Published 2008 | 245 Pages | $14.95
    ISBN: 978-0-9796177-3-7

Robert Crosson, *Daybook (1983–86)*
    Published 2011 | 96 Pages | $12.95
    ISBN-13: 978-0-9845289-1-2
    ISBN- 0-9845289-1-1

Mohammed Dib, *Tlemcen or Places of Writing*
    Published 2012 | 120 pages | $12.95
    ISBN-13: 978-0-9845289-7-4
    ISBN-10: 0-9845289-7-0

Ray DiPalma, *The Ancient Use of Stone:*
Journals and Daybooks, 1998–2008
    Published 2009 | 216 pages | $14.95
    ISBN: 978-0-9796177-5-1

Ray DiPalma, *Obedient Laughter*
    Published 2014 | 144 pages | $12.95
    ISBN: 978-0-9860173-3-9

Jean-Michel Espitallier, *Espitallier's Theorem*
Translated from the French by Guy Bennett
    Published 2003 | 137 pages | $12.95
    ISBN: 0-9755924-2-4

Leland Hickman, *Tiresias: The Collected Poems of Leland Hickman*
    Published 2009 | 205 Pages | $14.95
    ISBN: 978-0-9822645-1-5

Norman M. Klein, *Freud in Coney Island and Other Tales*
    Published 2006 | 104 pages | $12.95
    ISBN: 0-9755924-6-7

Luxorius, *Opera Omnia or, a Duet for Sitar and Trombone*
    Published 2012 | 216 pages | $12.95
    ISBN-13: 978-0-9845289-6-7
    ISBN-10: 0-9845289-5-4

Ken McCullough, *Left Hand*
    Published 2004 | 191 pages | $12.95
    ISBN: 0-9755924-1-6

Béatrice Mousli, Editor, *Review of Two Worlds:*
French and American Poetry in Translation
    Published 2005 | 148 pages | $12.95
    ISBN: 0-9755924-3-2

Laura Mullen, *Enduring Freedom*
    Published 2012 | 80 Pages | $12.95
    ISBN-13: 978-0-9845289-8-1
    ISBN-10: 0-9845289-8-9

Ryan Murphy, *Down with the Ship*
    Published 2006 | 66 pages | $12.95
    ISBN: 0-9755924-5-9

Aldo Palazzeschi, *The Arsonist*
Translation from the Italian by Nicholas Benson
    Published 2013 | 232 pages | $12.95
    ISBN: 978-0-9845289-9-8

Dennis Phillips, *Navigation: Selected Poems, 1985–2010*
    Published 2011 | 288 pages | $14.95
    ISBN-13: 978-0-9845289-4-3
    ISBN: 0-9845289-4-6

Antonio Porta, *Piercing the Page: Selected Poems 1958–1989*
    Published 2011 | 368 pages | $14.95
    ISBN-13: 978-0-9845289-5-0
    ISBN: 0-9845289-5-4

Eric Priestley, *For Keeps*
    Published 2009 | 264 pages | $12.95
    ISBN: 978-0-979-6177-4-4

Sophie Rachmuhl, *A Higher Form of Politics: the Rise of a Poetry Scene,
Los Angeles, 1950-1990*
Translated from the French by Mindy Menjou & George Drury Smith
    Published 2014 | 352 pages | $12.95
    ISBN-13: 978-0-9860173-5-3
    ISBN-10: 0-9860173-5-3

Ari Samsky, *The Capricious Critic*
    Published 2010 | 240 pages | $12.95
    ISBN-13: 978-0-979-177-6-8
    ISBN: 0-979-6177-6-6

Hélène Sanguinetti, *Hence This Cradle*
Translated from the French by Ann Cefola
    Published 2007 | 160 pages | $12.95
    ISBN: 970-0-9755924-7-2

Janet Sarbanes, *Army of One*
    Published 2008 | 173 pages | $12.95
    ISBN-13: 978-0-9796177-1-3
    ISBN-10: 0-9796177-1-5

Severo Sarduy, *Beach Birds*
Translated from the Spanish by Suzanne Jill Levine and Carol Maier
    Published 2007 | 182 pages | $12.95
    ISBN: 978-9755924-8-9

Adriano Spatola, *The Porthole*
Translated from the Italian by Beppe Cavatorta and Polly Geller
>   Published 2011 | 112 pages | $12.95
>   ISBN-13: 978-0-9796177-9-9
>   ISBN-10: 0-9796177-9-0

Adriano Spatola, *Toward Total Poetry*
Translated from the Italian by Brendan W. Hennessey and
Guy Bennett, with an Introduction by Guy Bennett
>   Published 2008 | 176 pages | $12.95
>   ISBN-13: 978-0-9796177-2-0
>   ISBN-10: 0-9796177-3-1

Carol Treadwell, *Spots and Trouble Spots*
>   Published 2004 | 176 pages | $12.95
>   ISBN: 0-9755924-0-8

Paul Vangelisti, *Wholly Falsetto with People Dancing*
>   Published 2013 | 136 pages | $12.95
>   ISBN-13: 978-0-980173-0-8
>   ISBN: 0-9860173-0-2

Allyssa Wolf, *Vaudeville*
>   Published 2006 | 82 pages | $12.95
>   ISBN: 0-9755924-4-0a